Pause

By the same author

Unclutter Your Life: Transforming Your Physical, Mental, and Emotional Space
(translated internationally)

Pause

Putting the Brakes on a Runaway Life

Katherine Gibson

INSOMNIAC PRESS

Library and Archives Canada Cataloguing in Publication

Gibson, Katherine, 1951-

Pause : putting the brakes on a runaway life / Katherine Gibson.

ISBN 1-897178-23-9 (pbk.)

    1. Simplicity. 2. Quality of life. I. Title.

HQ2037.G43 2006   646.7   C2006-903485-0

The publisher gratefully acknowledges the support of the Canada Council, the Ontario Arts Council, and the Department of Canadian Heritage through the Book Publishing Industry Development Program.

Printed and bound in Canada

Insomniac Press, 192 Spadina Avenue, Suite 403
Toronto, Ontario, Canada, M5T 2C2
www.insomniacpress.com

Permissions

Ocean Alexander: The First 25 Years by Marianne Scott. Ocean Alexander Marine, 2006. Quoted with permission of the authors.

www.healthandyoga.com quoted with permission of the website authors.

Your Garagenous Zone by Bill West. Paragon Garage Company Ltd., 2004. Quoted with permission of the author.

For Bob Unwin
my best buddy

and

the Willows Beach walker
whose "pause" inspired this book

Contents

Thanks to You ...

Creating a book is akin to giving birth. First comes the conception (the fun part), then the gestation, and finally the delivery. Many hands have helped to bring this baby to life and each has left its mark; I thank you all. A dozen muffins for Jed Stuart, who many years ago encouraged me to write a little article about Sark. Special hugs to my dear friend and colleague Marianne Scott, who has crossed dozens of my t's throughout the years. A high-five to Irene Roy and Barbara Dunnett, my sisters-of-the-heart, and to Lynn Van Bakel for her puffs, poofs, and constant encouragement. A huge thanks to my PWAC colleagues who shared their small indulgences with me. A special thank you to my literary agent Carolyn Swayze for her TLC, and to publisher Michael O'Connor and the staff at Insomniac for their can-do attitude. As always, I treasure the angelic guidance of Sally, Agnes, and Francis.

The experiences, expertise, and generosity of many talented people are woven throughout *Pause*. Heartfelt thanks to Barbara Ballard, Robert Bateman, Bill Barazzuol, Sister Patricia Shreenan, Jimmy Gibson, Bonnie Carter, Linda Kavelin Popov, Carolyn Bateman, Steve MacDowall, Linda

Chu, Dr. Margaret Nix, Lorraine Cummings, Hans Schmid and the Right to Quiet Society, Mark Sichel, Charles Herman, Tanya Gulliver, Nadina Schaddelee, Jeremy Unwin, Deborah Millar, Sherry Irvine, Kit Caldwell, Sandy Smith, Leanne Fenez, Ann Douglas, Valerie Sovran Mitchell, Sue Johnson, Harald Koehn, Gary Howell, Linda Miller, Jan Godsmark, Harriet Kendrick, Robert Kendrick, Duane Lecky, Murray Harrison, Brad Stokes and the Kindness Crew, Rosie Smyth, Bruce Wilson, Quiet Garden Trust, Don Monet, Carmen Lassooij, Nicole Ingram, Jodi DeLong, Helen Chesnut, Terrance Williams, Renée Lessard, Brit's Pub, Bud Carmichael, Wendy Bumgardner, Miriam Weinstein, Stanley Coren, Doreen Home, Sandra O'Leary, Maia Gibb, Judith Stock, Shivon Robinsong, Denis Donnelly, Sharon Begg, Hart Sugarman, Barbara Carlson, Marion Cumming, Pat Zanichelli, Eileen MacNeil, Lucinda Vardey, Michelle Greysen, and Linda Mason Hunter.

We should all do what in the long run gives us joy,
even if it is only picking grapes or sorting the laundry.
— E. B. White, author

Why Pause?

Quite simply, the runaway life is doing us in.

Have we become time slaves?

We charge through life with bags under our eyes, pills in our pockets, and sadness in our hearts. From the bolt out the door at sunrise, we hammer through the day until we plop into bed. And then, up we get to do it again. Lunch is a sandwich in one hand and a phone in the other. When the sun sets, we turn ourselves upside down entertaining instead of relaxing. Exercise is scheduled with military precision and sleep is for wimps. Eating disorders, depression, sleep deprivation, and techno-overload have become the hallmarks of everyday life. We are rushing down a perilous path, hellbent on a runaway life, and we are doing it in droves.

Like many of us, I embraced the world as a happening place, bustling with people, noise, and plenty of action. Although I spend long periods of time writing, my speaking and workshop engagements frequently take me away from home. It is a thrill to share thoughts about my work, and interacting with people around the country is intensely satisfying. But as the requests increased, I was sleeping less and working more, entrapped in my own version of a runaway life, bouncing from one commitment to another, touching down just long enough to take off again. Although I give lectures about life management and have written a book on balanced living, I had slipped into high gear and there I stayed. I had become like the plumber whose taps dripped.

During this time, my youngest brother contracted a serious illness. As the life of this witty, talented, and beautiful young father hovered between heaven and Earth, I broke out in a rash doctors could not explain. My senses numbed as days dissolved one into the other. Although I could *see* the beauty around me, I could not *feel* it. Yet I pressed on, even as I inched towards physical, emotional, and spiritual burnout.

One evening my angels intervened in the form of a most improbable messenger. I was at the Toronto airport waiting for takeoff on an evening flight. The seats next to mine were unoccupied and I crossed my fingers they would stay that way. Then, with just minutes to spare, a young man shot down the aisle.

"Hi," he said brightly. "I'm Andrew. You've got me for the next five hours!" I braced myself, gave him a nice-to know-you-but-please-don't-bother-me smile, and went back to a project I was reviewing. When we were in the air and the booze cart appeared, he turned to me and said, "Can I buy you a drink?" I hesitated, eyeing the thick wad of notes in front of me. "Hey, don't make me drink alone," he quipped with an impish grin before I could reply. Perhaps a wee nip would be okay and I acquiesced. He ordered and then, without any prompting, launched into a torrent of stories about new Toronto restaurants, nightclubs, and his mad dashes from late-night parties to early-morning business appointments. "I'm out all the time," he continued at a feverish pace. "Can't stay home. Might miss something." After he had chronicled his whirlwind social life, he hesitated before adding that he would like a relationship someday, "when I get the time."

Andrew reminded me of a whippet wired for the next race. He was fidgety and constantly fingered his cellphone ("I live with this thing. It never leaves me. Even when I sleep.") He ordered more drinks, which, I insisted, he would have to manage himself. Andrew, the man who could not stop spinning, was just twenty-seven. I wondered if he would make twenty-eight.

As the plane flew west, the middle-aged man across the aisle worked on his laptop. Beside him, a woman pored over a briefcase bulging with files, and next to her a beautifully groomed fashionista looking jittery and impatient flipped through the in-flight magazine. They all appeared tired, worn-out, and stressed. In them, I saw Andrew—and I saw myself.

When I returned home, I began questioning why we push so hard at life. Where are we rushing to, and what do we expect to find when we get there? I saw us spinning out of control like children on a playground carousel, unable to stop. With these thoughts in my head, an exhausting schedule behind me, and visions of Andrew fresh in my mind, I unpacked my bags. I'd had enough. I put everything but my non-negotiable commitments on hold. I needed to rest, read, and think.

The weeks passed and time slowed. I took life on in bite-sized morsels and savored its subtleties. I began to walk every day. At first I did it as therapy, knowing it was good for me. Then I began to look forward to these mini-escapes and out I would go, whatever the weather. During these strolls I thought about the crazy-making way we live.

I turned to the wisdom of others and tuned into The Voice that speaks to us all if we slow down long enough to listen. What I heard was a single, simple word: *pause*.

This word haunted me. I liked its gentle sound and quiet strength. It brought to mind patience, mindfulness, and discernment—qualities that resonate throughout a thoughtful and considered approach to life. I realized it is wise to care for ourselves as lovingly as we would a child, yet doing this is easily overlooked and can even seem self-indulgent. As I continued to contemplate this, I came to understand that we might not know we are in a pressure cooker until we are out. I also saw that stepping back from the fray and taking daily pauses is an "essential service" we must do for ourselves and is at the core of a creative, vibrant life. Whether it is to take five minutes to stretch at our desk, play catch with the kids, or sit in a park during lunch hour, I learned that putting the brakes on our runaway lives will help ensure we drive our own lives, and do not crash into barriers of exhaustion, confusion, and chaos.

After consulting experts in health care, spirituality, and psychology, and spending time with others who graciously shared their experiences, I realized it matters little *what* we do, it is the *why* that counts. I also learned we are useless to others and ourselves if we are physical and emotional wrecks.

While some of us are so overwhelmed we might be tempted to "pull a Thoreau" and disappear into our personal Walden Pond, many of us do not want radical change, but rather a less hectic, more manageable journey. Whatever our position in society, whatever commitments we face, whatever the complexities of our personal challenges, we *can* create a life that soothes our souls; we can do *less* with *more* passion and weed out the time-suckers that drain our energy. It is a matter of choice. Running ourselves ragged does not have to be in the program.

Pause: Putting the Brakes on a Runaway Life is not an analysis of the chaos that churns within our complex society, but a gentle nudge to inject moments of fun, adventure, self-care, and serenity into the day. I hope to convince you that life dramatically improves when we eliminate meaningless activities, back-to-back commitments, and unfulfilling obligations to make room for things that gives life zest.

Pause consists of four sections that explore our spiritual and earthly realms. Each chapter focuses on one theme and ends with *Pause to Ponder*, a collection of thoughts to help you create your own very personal pauses.

I learned through my own period of chaos that when we tune up our soul we tune up our life. Since lasting change starts inside us and radiates outward, the book opens with *Inner Pauses*. The chapters in this section offer introspective, spiritual elements to bring a sense of peace into the day. They explore the very real world of the spirit and show us how to dance and sing with our angels.

Next we examine *Everyday Pauses*, the vital elements of living well. These chapters suggest ways to incorporate life-enhancing activities into each day. And, yes, you will find time for these because I hope to convince you that they form the foundation of a happy life.

The book then turns to *Playful Pauses*. These range from a discussion of special relationships—a "sweet pause" is much more than just dessert—to the delights of small indulgences and such joys as poking about a garden and spoiling ourselves rotten.

The book's final section, *Welcome Home*, explains how to create a perfect place to pause, a sanctuary from the hectic outside world, tailor-made just for us. It provides strate-

gies for creating a calm, uncluttered, and intensely personal home space. Through stories and comments from
experts, we will consider suggestions to make our home a
haven, a refuge for retreat and renewal.

At the end of the book, you will find a list of resources
that have influenced the ideas presented here. I have also
included a list of *quick pauses*, suggestions for spontaneous
mini-breaks.

I wrote *Pause* for all of us. Whether we work from
home, slog it out at the office, in a classroom, hospital, or
factory, or are retired, life can get ahead of us—if we let it.
Cooking with the kids, watching the snow fall on a
Saturday afternoon, escaping on mini-retreats, and shame-
lessly enjoying daily delights remind us that joy is an accu-
mulation of happy moments. I hope this book inspires you
to contemplate a pause from the runaway life, if only for a
few minutes a day.

So, put up your feet.
Take a deep breath.
Pause awhile.

All good wishes,

Katherine Gibson
www.katherinegibson.com

Inner Pauses ...

connect us to our sense of self

Every day can be a grand party if we pause and step aside from the rush of the runaway life. The chapters in this section take us off the freeways of hurried living onto subdued sideroads where goodness, gentleness, and all the blessings of human experience thrive. We will take trips to the heart and learn the secrets of the inner pause—for when we do, life's discord transforms into a sweet symphony of color, texture, and harmony.

Dancing with Angels

When we pause to summon our inner guidance,
life sparkles with possibilities.

*I take a break during a conference I am attending to stroll on
the beach near the hotel. It is a perfect California day, all sunny
and cloudless. As I make my way along the promenade, I notice a
young man kneeling in the sand, surrounded by a pile of stones,
strategically placing them one on top of the other. How strange to
see a grown man playing with rocks, but this is trendy Laguna
Beach where the unusual is quite normal. "I'm creating art,"
says this balancer-of-stones when I stop to speak with him. I learn
he is also a home-grown philosopher. "Rock art is like life," he
tells me. "It is temporary and requires a series of balances and
counterbalances. And it is a meditation, a way of focusing—an
opening into my creative center."*

*His comments intrigue me. I pick up a stone from among
those lying around him and run my hand against its roughness.
Another feels smooth, almost silky. Before long, I kick off my
shoes and, with sand between my toes, begin my own humble
attempt at rock-balancing. The noises on the beach recede as I
enter his world and feel a sense of exceeding calm.*

*Rock-balancing, I learn, is an exercise in choosing priorities.
And it is about patience. As I contemplate one rock and then*

another, I begin to understand why he sees them as metaphors for the human condition:

    The small or insignificant can be vital to success.

    The large or dominant can either support or destroy.

    Nothing we create is permanent.

    Time can seem to stand still.

    Quiet is good.

    So is persistence.

    Heaven might be a rocky beach.

    Our next teacher could be wearing a nose ring, sandals, and beach shorts.

Behold, the morning sprint! With alarm clocks as our starting pistols, we fire out of bed, toss on our clothes, gulp a coffee, and charge out the door. As we dash through the day, the hours evaporate until, gosh, it is time to start over. But imagine a gentle beginning when we rise slowly, take in the early morning freshness, and pause. That is the time to ruminate on who we are, why we do what we do, and whether our world is turning as it should. Is our work fulfilling? Are we using our talents to serve others and light up the world? Are we living our best possible life? What blessing has the day already given us? It is a time for grace and being graceful, a time to take charge of the day and not let it take charge of us.

Making time for contemplation, to dance with our angels, is an essential inner pause. Some call it prayer, others meditation. Some see it simply as time alone. Whether we follow a religious ritual, a wisdom tradition, or an individual form of reflection, a contemplative interlude sets us up for the day, giving us an internal grounding to handle the challenges of our outer world.

Although the quintessential scientist, the brilliant Albert Einstein said that "when you examine the lives of the most influential people who have ever walked among us, you discover they have been aligned first with their spiritual nature and only then with their physical selves." He might then agree that pausing to dance with our angels (or whatever we choose to call our intuitive or God-given guidance) summons a vast and powerful force that waltzes us from one adventure to another.

And, while they are wise and caring, angels also have a wild sense of humor and love it when we laugh with them. They always know what is best for us and they are always waiting outside our door. Letting them in to play with us is to embark on a journey filled with synchronicity, guidance we can trust, and fun. But they are terribly polite and won't come knocking. We must invite them in. But how?

Just Ask

My friend Bill is an inspiring example of how communing with angels led to clarity that triggered a life-altering choice. He had a passion for all things ancient, especially the dynasties of Egypt. He made a trip there, floating down the Nile, even sleeping on a pyramid under the stars (which did not amuse the guards who unceremoniously booted him out). Although he is of Italian descent, he left Egypt knowing this land spoke to his soul—it was his "bone country." It would be three decades before he returned.

Bill became a respected teacher of western civilization, yet knew he was not living his *right* life, but was caught in one that deadened his spirit. Eventually, with a marriage behind him and his kids grown-up, he was free to explore a new direction. Yet what should that be?

Although he was a spiritual man, he now made more time to pause and summon his inner wisdom. When his angels gave him the go-ahead, he listened, and when the time was right, he pulled up stakes and headed east.

Bill is now teaching in Alexandria and has become a recognized scholar specializing in Egypt's intriguing history. "When we live in harmony with what is right for us, life is truly blissful," he says. "I took a magic carpet ride and look where I am! I have a dream life in a country that resonates deeply inside me." But to find it, Bill spent long hours contemplating, praying, and meditating. It worked—brilliantly. Bill trusted the power of prayer. It was a pause that changed his life.

Celebrating God Is Good Medicine

The ritual of pausing for morning contemplation is as ancient as sun worship. But as today's secular life swirls in a busy vortex, the ancient traditions of prayer, meditation, and quiet time—whatever we choose to call it—become all the more important.

While the spiritual benefits of meditation are acknowledged, according to *www.healthandyoga.com*, medical studies suggest we benefit physically as well.

Meditative practices:
• decrease respiratory rate
• increase blood flow and slow heart rate
• increase exercise tolerance
• regulate blood pressure
• reduce anxiety by lowering the levels of blood lactate
• decrease pain due to tension and headaches
• increase serotonin, which can reduce depression, obesity, insomnia, and headaches
• increase the activity of "natural-killer cells" which attack harmful bacteria and cancer cells.

Imagine infusing the body with all those advantages before breakfast! It gets better if we pray or meditate with others. More than 1,200 studies and 400 reviews from Canada, Europe, and the United States show that pausing for a little pew-time is dynamite for body and soul. Those who regularly attend religious services live on average up to seven years longer than those who do not. Non-attendees are twice as likely to die of digestive diseases and have more incidents of cardiovascular disease and respiratory illnesses.

Studies at universities in Utah, California, and Alberta show that Mormons are relatively free of cancer. A Danish study indicates Adventist men have lower than average rates of colon and bladder cancer. Male members of the Old Order of Amish between the ages of forty and sixty-nine had a 35 percent lower rate of circulatory diseases than non-Amish men of the same age. [1]

Turning and Twisting

Heavenly voices speak to us in the most unusual circumstances—even when we are standing on our heads. While yoga's sexy poses get all the attention, anyone can do the simple stretches that point the way to heaven. Many yoga poses have been adapted for beginners and those with physical limitations. Tai Chi, another form of moving meditation, is terrific (and easy). Both offer workouts that tone the body *and* clear the "mind-field," encouraging us to breath slowly and deeply, keeping our thoughts in the moment while gently easing out the clutter of negative energy generated by such feelings as worry, guilt, and anger.

Charles, a college professor who lives in the Wisconsin

countryside, rises when it is still dark to do meditative yoga, a discipline he has followed most of his adult life. He credits this body-soul regime for "helping me deal with the stresses of the day, keep a limber body, and connect spiritually to the oneness of all creation." It seems to be working, because he is edging toward his mid-sixties yet looks a decade younger.

Ancient Symbol Lures New Age Disciples

We most often associate meditative activities with stillness. But movement can also summon our angels. Prayer walking is a contemplative experience that stretches back to early European monastic, Buddhist, and other Eastern traditions. Today, Linus Mundy, a follower of a monastic discipline, gently encourages and elegantly explains the wisdom in "taking a stroll with your soul." Mundy calls this practice prayer walking and sees it as the antidote to today's obsession with "going fast, saving time, and doing more."

Walking labyrinths has moved beyond its religious origins to become a popular tool for stilling the busy mind, finding balance, and stimulating insight. Perhaps the best-known labyrinth lies inside the glorious twelfth-century Chartres Cathedral, an hour southwest of Paris. Today there are labyrinths in medical centers, parks, churches, schools, prisons, memorial parks, retreat centers, and on private property.

A labyrinth is a circuitous pathway that can really juice up an introspective experience. Unlike a maze, which has tricks and dead ends, a labyrinth has a clear entry point, then circles toward the center (denoted with a symbol such as a six-petal flower, a cross, or chalice), and then leads out.

"[A labyrinth] is a path of prayer, a walking meditation, a crucible of change, a watering hole for the spirit, and a mirror of the soul," writes the Rev. Dr. Lauren Artress, Director of Veriditas: The Worldwide Labyrinth Project.[2] "The person walking a labyrinth uses the same path to enter and to return. Generally there are three stages to the walk: releasing on the way in, receiving in the center, and returning, that is, taking back out into the world that which you have received. There is no right way or wrong way to walk a labyrinth."

Nadina, who is recovering from a debilitating neurological condition, finds contemplative peace by walking a labyrinth that is painted on the driveway of her home. "I was introduced to the labyrinth through *Walking a Sacred Path*, a book I got as a birthday present. There was a labyrinth close to where I live, so I tried it out and felt a resonance with it from the beginning. Now I walk it as a personal meditation, as a family ritual for peace at Christmas, and with others who are attracted to it."

Three Stages of Walking a Labyrinth

Walking a labyrinth is a powerful experience that does not require training or have rules.

The Journey In moves us from the concrete world into the spiritual world as we exchange busy thoughts and emotions for quiet and stillness.

Enlightenment occurs at the center where we can pray or meditate and be open to insight into whatever we need to understand.

The Journey Out is an experience of melding the spiritual with the practical, putting our insights to work in our daily lives.

Prayer Walking

While some will use a labyrinth to focus their meditation, Linda Kavelin Popov simply walks. She and her husband Dan are co-founders of The Virtues Project, a power-ful, global initiative that focuses on the virtues valued throughout many cultures and sacred traditions.[3] Linda, who wrote *A Pace of Grace: The Virtues of a Sustainable Life,* travels throughout North America, Europe, Asia, Australia, and New Zealand. Wherever she goes, no matter how packed her day might be, she sets aside time to walk with her angels.

"I get a profound sense of connection with Spirit when I walk in a place of beauty," says the post-polio syndrome survivor. She credits this simple interlude as a key to maintaining her physical and spiritual balance. "Like many of us, I spend long hours at the computer. Leaving the house for a walk, especially one that goes uphill, gets me breathing deeply, something I do not do when I sit. I focus on being in the moment, being really present to what's around me. That's when I get my most inspira-tional messages and visions."

Listen to Your Guru

While our angels like to hold center stage, they also speak to us through the words of others. But we do not need to flock to an ashram to kneel at the foot of a guru. Our teachers might be building rock sculptures on the beach or having a beer at the neighborhood pub. They might come into our life for a brief few hours or stay for a lifetime. If we pay attention, we will find a special guru meant just for us, however unlikely he or she may seem.

I have often marveled at how someone will enter my life when I need them. Some years ago when I moved to a new city and was looking for work as a teacher, I just hap-pened to meet someone in my particular area of specializa-tion who was taking a maternity leave. Presto! I had a job!

Later, when I wrestled with a difficult family problem, another angel came knocking to offer incredible insight and wisdom that resolved the situation. If we pause and consider the people we have known, even for a short time, we might realize they have been "temporary angels" who significantly smoothed our life's journey.

Journaling and Pajamas

Greeting or ending the day snuggled in pajamas with paper and pen can also be a powerful meditative pause. Recording our thoughts lets us express random ideas and work through feelings. Journaling is an internal sorting-out, a release of interior turbulence. We might create poems, pose questions, write affirmations, or wander through visualizations. These very personal records permit us to review our thoughts over a period of time and consider themes that emerge. They are insightful tools to articulate what's on our mind without self-judgment or criticism. Over time, committing issues to paper often leads to clarity.

Our guru might also speak to us from the pages of a book. A friend may give us one that contains a message we find powerful and life-changing (as *Walking a Sacred Path* was for Nadina). Sometimes, a volume finds us. Pay attention, for books that *just happen* to pop into your life may be gifts from your angels with messages meant for you. One morning I saw an unfamiliar book on the kitchen table. My husband, who had chanced upon it, had left it for me with the toast and jam. It was the ideal volume for the morning's quiet time. My husband was so thoughtful to share this little gem with me.

Nix the Narcissism

Edouard Manet's *Bathers on the Seine* depicts a woman sitting naked on a rock before a river. A lush forest rises behind her. Her arms are raised, circling her head. Her breasts are small but her belly and thighs suggest a woman of substance. She gazes outward, not with sensuality or shame, but with the eyes of a dreamer at peace with herself. In the background another woman stands with her back toward us. She too is naked, and, as with her companion, her ample buttocks are supported by solid, fleshy thighs. These beautiful subjects embody the fullness of womanhood in the mid-1800s. Angels? Perhaps. Twiggy girl-women they are certainly not.

How times have changed! Manet's dimpled darlings with their bountiful bellies and thunder thighs might have been hotties in the days of petticoats and button-up boots, but they would be non-starters in today's version of cool. Rather than spend afternoons idling by a river, we are more apt to be pumping iron, consulting body-contouring experts, or herding into gyms (or onto surgeons' tables) in search of creaseless, perfect bodies. "I'm going to fight the age thing with everything I've got," says one thirtyish woman as she wedges fitness programs and reshaping consultations into her already busy schedule.

She's not alone.

And no wonder: selling "cool" is a billion-dollar industry that thrives on creating insecurity. It takes the strength of Samson to ignore the billboards, TV shows, and magazine advertisements that so insidiously influence how we feel about ourselves. Who we *are* is being eclipsed by how we *look*. The more we move our focus from inside to outside, the more we erode our peace of mind.

Like every creature that inhabits the Earth, we are constantly changing, maturing, and will eventually die. Yet our culture is obsessed with staying young. Many of us take excessive interest in our own appearance. Humorist

Dave Barry notes that more money is being spent on breast implants and Viagra than on Alzheimer's research. "This means that by 2030, there should be a large elderly population with perky boobs and huge erections and absolutely no recollection of what to do with them!" Though he chuckles, the issue is no laughing matter.

How often do we pause to consider that growing old is not a disease, but a privilege denied to many? No matter how much we spend on rejuvenating wonder-products, we *will* age. And just think of the hours spent primping and prodding and poking and pumping—hours we cannot recapture, no matter how important or rich we are. We might have used this time to build a tree fort with the kids, knit sweaters for the homeless, or just pause and chat with our angels.

Staying Cool

Certainly our self-esteem is bolstered when we feel good about our appearance, but the acceptance of maturity ought to conquer the urge to compete with magazine models. Buying and interpreting cool is a full-time job— one we pile on top of our hectic agendas. With the goalposts continually shifting ("the look" is as fickle as a woman who swears off chocolate), staying cool is confusing and takes Olympian commitment. New products, hairstyles, decisions to wax or not to wax, unpredictable hemline lengths and collar styles keep us broke, anxious, and very, very busy.

In January 1993, I caught a television program about Audrey Hepburn, a real-life angel who had just died of colorectal cancer at age sixty-three. Among the many images shown was film footage of her in Somalia, a poor and dangerous country on the east coast of Africa. Although she could have been basking on a yacht in the Mediterranean, she was touring a drought-ravaged village as an ambassador for UNICEF on a hot, dusty day.

Her quiet, determined commitment to the children of Somalia was inspiring, but her face was unforgettable, though it showed her advancing years. The lines that framed the almond eyes and crisscrossed her face highlighted her integrity, making her delicate beauty all the more lovely. This darling of the big screen took Oscar Wilde's quip that "a man's face is his autobiography and a woman's face is a work of fiction" and turned it on its head.

Audrey Hepburn had many accomplishments to her credit, but perhaps one of the most memorable is that she lived her life head-on and let it show. To me, this made her *really* cool.

While time in front of the mirror has its place, time for inner reflection allows space to ponder, percolate and divide, and ultimately reassemble our thoughts. Whether we begin the day with an hour-long yoga session, a ten-minute walk in the park, or a few moments to write or read, making time to dance with our angels will ground and center us. Seeing oneself as okay whatever one's age—and accepting that the truly beautiful (and memorable) person exudes confidence and personal style—will give us permission to step aside from a runaway life, pause, and welcome every stage of our earthly existence with wonder and anticipation. And when we do, we will have time to sip tea in the sun, play in the garden, ride a bike, spend a day with someone special, or sit in undisturbed contemplation. Leg-waxing and eyebrow-plucking cannot compare with that.

Pause to Ponder
- How can you make time for daily contemplation?
- How can you develop a daily ritual that fits with your spiritual or religious tradition?
- Are you on your right path, igniting your passions?
- Are you living a life that is in harmony with your values?
- Where would you like to be if you had no obstacles?
- Are these obstacles real or imagined? What steps can you take to nudge them out of the way?
- To what extent do you look inwards and set your own definition of beauty?
- How does comparing yourself to others undermine your true worth?
- Do pressures make you feel outdated and inadequate? How can you resist them?

Gratitude's Gift

As the need for more diminishes,
appreciation for what we have grows.

April should have been sitting with the other students instead of climbing up on my lap. But I'm glad she did, for she gave me a hug of such intense happiness. I can feel her thin arms around me now, even though this happened several years ago.

In her hand she clutched a purple ribbon stamped with the word "Participant" that all the youngsters in the school were given to celebrate Track and Field Day. A handful of the most athletic children received ribbons of red, yellow, and blue. But to April, her ordinary ribbon was just perfect.

That day, this nine-year old girl, who was mentally challenged and suffered from cerebral palsy, gave me a gift of striking simplicity. Her absolute joy taught me the power of appreciating what we have.

Our Cup Is Running Over

Even a quick inventory of the good things we take for granted could fill a day: libraries packed with books, videos, and music all free for the asking; cars and buses that can whip us from one town to the next; jets that can speed us from Seattle to San Diego for lunch and back. We have dishwashers, cellphones, cheap long-distance phone rates, and exotic foods from around the world waiting at the corner store. But even with these blessings and many, many more, our happiness quotient is anything but healthy. We are popping antidepressants in record numbers as we work ourselves silly in an attempt to buy our bits of bliss. Yet religious leaders, philosophers, mystics, and Eastern gurus agree that the quickest road to fulfillment is not to load up on the next new thing, but to pause and count our blessings—to *desire* what we already *have*.

Several years ago, I spent an evening with a friend who had left her marriage some months earlier. Her children were very young, she could find only part-time work, and things weren't going well with her estranged husband. Life for her looked bleak and she felt despondent and defeated. While we sipped tea, she continued ranting. Suddenly she said, "Hey, it's not all bad. At least I have a couch to sit on."

"You're right, and there's a rug under the couch."

"And a floor under the rug."

"We've got tea to drink."

"With milk."

"And sugar."

"And a bowl to put the sugar in."

Before long, we were giggling like silly schoolgirls. We could have spent the rest of the night listing the things we owned, the kindnesses we had been shown, the opportunities we had, our good health, and the super people who supported us when we needed them. In counting our blessings, we realized we were inundated with them. I have thought of that evening several times since, and of young April.

Appreciating what we have dramatically transforms how we live. So much of the angst we feel is generated by the competitive thrust of our get-everything-fast culture. The pressure to measure success by the standard of our celebrity-obsessed popular media is all too pervasive. *More* feeds dissatisfaction; it muscles out the pleasures of the present and pushes us into the uncertain realm of tomorrow. *More* entices us to upgrade the kitchen countertops and rush out to catch the Saturday sales; it chews up our time, depletes our wallets, and exhausts our spirit. Pausing to count our blessings and to plunge into a sea of gratitude will outfox this voracious beast and give us a free, never-ending supply of contentment.

A friend shared this scenario he encountered in the elevator of an office building early one morning. The day was a wet one with rain slithering everywhere. When the elevator door opened he saw an older gentleman who was leaning on a cane. My friend nodded to the man, stepped in to join him, and said, "It sure is a lousy day out there."

"Oh," said the older man. "I think it's a pretty good day."

"But it's pissing rain."

The man laughed quietly as the elevator reached his stop, and then he said, "Son, each day I can get up in the morning, look into the mirror, and see this ugly face looking back, is not a good day—it's a great day!"

This awareness—being tuned into the good things around us—so often fades into the wallpaper of life. For someone who is ill or struggling with advancing age, just getting up in the morning is a cause for celebration. Being able to see, walk, and hear are blessings easily overlooked until we are groping in the dark or being fitted with a cane or hearing aid. Having one good friend who sincerely cares for us is as priceless as the Hope Diamond.

A Positive Pause

Cultivating optimism, the right hand of gratitude, helps us cope with the inevitable challenges in our common human journey. Those who betray or act maliciously towards others can highlight goodness in those who don't. Job loss can open new possibilities. Financial misfortune can lead to new priorities. Illness gives us a deeper insight into the fragility of existence.

Death can jolt us into forging a more profound relationship with life. Some years ago the London *Sunday Times* ran a short feature on Dennis Potter, a pillar of the British television industry who died in 1994 from pancreatic cancer. The article explored how we might live if we knew, as Potter did, that death was imminent. Potter explained:

"Below my window the blossoms are out in full bloom now. Instead of seeing a nice blossom I see the whitest, frothiest, blossomyist blossom there ever could be. The newness of everything is absolutely wondrous. If you see in the present tense, boy, do you see it. And boy, can you celebrate it."

(I suggest you pause for a few seconds now, wherever you are, look out your window, *really* see what's there, and give thanks. It might be best pause of the day.)

The Power of Gratitude

Feeling grateful moves the heart (and is responsible for the little tingle you might have felt looking out your window), but *expressing* gratitude ignites the soul. How often do we pause to say thank you. Once a day? Once a week? Where once we wrote thank-you notes by hand, we now fire off quick e-mails. Our runaway lives leave little time for these small gestures of grace and good manners.

And of course, it is a good idea to pause to thank our

God. G. K. Chesterton, the prolific and enormously talented early-twentieth-century writer, once said, "You say grace before meals. All right. But I say grace before the concert and the opera; and grace before the play and pantomime; and grace before I open a book; and grace before sketching, painting, and swimming, fencing, boxing, walking, playing, dancing; and grace before I dip the pen in ink."

Thank-you Notes Are Nice

Sending a card to acknowledge a kindness is a simple but powerful act of gratitude. Think about picking up notecards in places you visit or making them with photographs you have taken. Here are a few occasions to adopt this considerate custom:
- After receiving a gift
- To acknowledge an overnight or weekend stay
- After a lunch or dinner held in your honor
- To recognize a special kindness
- Following a business interview

The flip side of gratitude is greed, an evil glutton that robs us of our chances for happiness by fueling our unattainable expectations. Greed is the architect of social disintegration, from failed relationships to war.

While greed is all too pervasive, we can bypass this dark downside. It is as simple as following young April's example: be it a prize on Track and Field Day, hot tea in a cup, a couch to sit on, or the joy of seeing our children's faces, if we pause to consider the goodness around us we'll be overwhelmed. We shall not only see, but *feel* those blessings.

Imagine a world with a daily "minute of gratitude." For sixty seconds each day, we would pause and count our blessings. The planet would be lit by billions of smiling faces and the world would become a gentler place for us all, as it did for me when a small girl climbed onto my lap clutching a purple ribbon, and gave me a great big hug.

Pause to Ponder

- What blessing do you have at this very moment? (Hint: If you are reading this, you have the blessing of sight and education. If you are being read to, someone cares very much for you.)
- What good things have come to you through unexpected difficult situations?
- Count your blessings every morning and watch life change dramatically. Think of those who picked the fruit you eat, pounded the nails in the floor you are standing on, and sewed the clothes you are wearing.
- Give thanks for rain, the soil, and the sun; you wouldn't be here without them.
- Give thanks for the people who have inspired or comforted you, toasted your highs and hugged you through the low times.

Extreme Kindness

Be kind, be caring, be thoughtful.
Watch life change!

Ted Harrison's paint-and-pause rhythm is as hypnotic as his glorious paintings of the Yukon. As I approach the door of his studio, I look through the window and can see him at work. He is sitting before an easel on a simple folding chair with his back to me. Even from outside, I can feel his intensity.

This icon of the Far North and one of Canada's most beloved artists is contemplating the canvas before him. Although he is expecting me, it is with regret that I interrupt this very intimate moment. He turns from his work and approaches me with an open, welcoming smile. His face is captivating, a lovely face, remarkably unlined for a man in his eighth decade.

He invites me into the studio I had so furtively observed when I first arrived. The room is bright and cheery. Lavender, red, fuchsia, and yellow paint covers the carpet below his workspace. Handmade cards from school children he has visited dangle from a line strung across one corner of the room. Citations and recognition plaques clutter the ledges. His paintings, radiating Christmas-morning joy, hang in spaces between the windows. Determined innocence marks each one.

"I saw horrible things during my military service," he says in the musical accent of his native County Durham in England.

"There is much darkness in the world, but peace and beauty can transform us. We are all capable of good and evil. We must choose good. When I returned home, I told myself, 'I shall paint only pleasant subjects. I shall paint kindness.'"

With those thoughts he contemplates his unfinished canvas. When it is complete, he will send it out into the world to become another measure of peace and beauty, a happy reminder that kindness can be a way of life.

There I was, jogging along a trail on a cold December day. A few minutes earlier, I had been sitting at home, feeling like a slug. But, because I try to spend time outdoors each day, I pulled on my sweats and out I went.

Other runners and walkers use this trail, but on that morning it seemed I was alone. And I was grumpy. When I rounded the bend, an elderly man walking his dog surprised me. As I trudged up beside him he called out brightly, "Good for you!" I grumbled, "It's work, not fun." When I was a few steps ahead of him, he shot back, "It'll get easier, lass. Just keep at it."

As I thought about those few words, I began to feel lighter and the run seemed easier. I jogged along, contemplating the short exchange. That sweet man did not know me. I was acting surly and aloof, and our paths might never cross again, but he took time to encourage a stranger. As with the best gestures of kindliness, his came straight from the heart without thought of personal payback. He did it for its own sake—*just because.*

The more I thought about that brief encounter, the more I realized how easy it is to be kind: a few words here, a smile there, and the light comes on in the person we touch.

No planning, discussions, meetings, or strategic strategies are needed, just the will to pause and gently connect.

Sharing a moment with someone who is troubled, making a quick I'm-thinking-of-you phone call, sending a funny card to a friend who needs a lift, or leaving flowers at the door where there has been a loss can suffuse another's life and our own with warmth. In a world filled with people barreling through life, a dash of thoughtfulness slows us down and lets us connect soul to soul. It confirms and strengthens our humanity.

Cool to Be Kind

In 2002, four young men from western Canada took a break from their everyday lives to load themselves into a motorhome and embark on The Extreme Kindness Tour, a three-month, cross-country excursion to commit "random acts of kindness" in as many communities as possible. They wanted to counter the senseless violence that dominated the daily news. They did not plan to do grand things, just scatter a little goodness into the world. From offering strangers cookies and making sandwiches for the marginalized, to spending the night with a homeless man in Fredericton and giving hugs on the streets of Toronto, the remarkable Val Litwin, Chris Bratseth, Brad Stokes, and Erik Hanson moved from one town to the next, spreading unconditional compassion.

"We knocked on doors to cook dinners, took kids out for a game of hockey, entertained at a children's hospital, and we gave away a lot of hugs," says Brad with a laugh. "Not everyone wants a hug from a stranger, but we had an 80-percent success rate. We even gave a big, tough Harley-Davidson-type guy a hug and he started to cry!"

He says that people often think the group wants money

or is trying to sell something. It is hard at first for people to accept that the men perform their "kindness pranks" just to bring a little fun and love into the world.

"My mother Judy inspired the project," says Brad. "She was incredible. Even when she was dying from cancer and near the end of her life, she thought about others. I remember looking for her in the hospital after a chemo treatment. After some searching, I found her reading to an older woman in another ward. I asked her why she didn't conserve her energy and think about herself. 'I have had so much given to me,' she said. 'This is what I have to do.' When she died, my best buddies and I knew we had to keep her spirit alive."

As Brad told his story, I thought of how his mother's selfless and caring nature now directs his life. The four-man crew has touched thousands through the books they have written, media appearances, speaking engagements, and impromptu offerings of kindness.

The power of compassion is hard to measure, yet it is enduring. The essence of Brad's mother lives in her son and his friends as they spread her gospel of love, and others, encouraged by their actions, spread their own brand of joy. What greater tribute to a woman who inspired a movement that spreads happiness wherever it goes.

Life is filled with blessings and grace is to be found everywhere. We need these things: we all are fighting a battle at some level and kindness provides the salve for the bruises and scrapes of life. It can appear as a brief, spontaneous gesture or a deliberate, purposeful act; it can bolster the soul of just one person or inspire a nation. Whatever form kindness takes, it has the potential to sustain, inspire, and empower. Pausing for kindness transcends the boundaries of age and cultures. Extending "gifts from the heart" opens the spirit to authentic communion with others. Whether our gestures are applauded or unappreciated, kindness is a potent, sustaining force.

Dr. Margaret Nix, a dear friend now in her mid-nineties and professor emerita at New York's Pace University, shared a story that underlines this theme. She spoke of a young girl who lived with her mother, a reclusive woman who had little passion for life and even less for maintaining a proper home. Even though the woman rarely left the house, she insisted her daughter attend Sunday school each week, which the child loved to do. One Sunday the girl was singled out by her teacher for excellent attendance and rewarded with a fresh rose. The girl was delighted and scampered home to show her mother.

The woman, caught up in her daughter's excitement, found a small bottle for a makeshift vase and put it on a table that was cluttered with dirty dishes and rumpled newspapers. They smiled, looked at each other, and then, seeing how the flower looked out of place, began to clear the table. Then they noticed the overcrowded counters and the grimy floor. Gradually they transformed their apartment into a home of immense pride. As these external changes took place, so did internal ones. Dr. Nix said the woman's life gradually improved, illustrating the ripple effect of a beautiful flower and a kind gesture.

We do not need to hop in a motorhome and tour the world to participate in Extreme Kindness. Spreading kindness does require action, though. The Random Acts of Kindness Foundation (*www.actsofkindness.org*) is doing just that. The website lists creative ideas for kids, adults, community groups, and schools. One woman organized her friends to paint the nails of the women living in a nursing home. Another gives birthday presents to the homeless. A group of young people staged a "drive-by flowering" in which they put flowers under the windshield wipers of cars on the street in the dead of night.

One day, my wise friend Lynn reminded me that while spreading kindness is something we do for others, we should not forget to be kind to ourselves. "Kindness starts with us," she said. "It's not selfish, it's essential. Wearing ourselves down pleasing or caring for others can hurt us emotionally if we feel unappreciated, and physically if we push aside our health. I'm living proof of that," she giggled as she suggested we take a "kind-to-me" pause and dig into a box of delicious, chocolate-covered coffee beans. Of course, I concurred!

Awakening kindness was the theme of an evening of music featuring Nawang Khechog, a former Buddhist monk who is now a celebrated composer and performer of Tibetan music. He considers kindness to be an inner jewel that lights our life wherever we go. And like Lynn, he also emphasized the importance of being good to ourselves. "The place where I live has wonderful vanilla ice cream," he said, referring to his home in Boulder, Colorado. "Every so often I treat myself. It's a small thing, but it reminds me that I must be kind to myself."

Spreading kindness confirms we are okay. Whatever personal foibles and shortcomings we may have, or whatever others may say about us, we know we have goodness in us. As Brad and the boys of the Extreme Kindness Tour say, "It feels so darn good when you make someone smile."

Cool Acts of Kindness

- Collect goods for a food bank
- Bring flowers to work and share them with co-workers
- Adopt a student who needs a friend, checking in periodically to see how things are going
- Buy a stranger a pizza
- Draw names at school or work, and have people bring a small gift for their secret pal
- Pay a compliment at least once a day
- Transport someone who cannot drive
- Mow a neighbor's grass
- Say something nice to everyone you meet today
- Send a treat to a school or day-care center
- Adopt a homeless pet at the humane society, or volunteer at a pet shelter
- Write a thank-you note to a mentor or someone who has influenced your life in a positive way
- Stop by a nursing home and visit a resident with no family nearby
- Give another driver your parking spot
- Tell your boss you think he/she does a good job
- Let your employees know how much you appreciate their work
- Tell a bus or taxi driver how much you appreciate their driving
- Drop off a plant, cookies, or doughnuts to the police or fire department
- Offer to return a shopping cart to the store for someone unloading groceries
- Send a letter to a former teacher, letting her know the difference she made in your life
- Send a gift anonymously to a friend
- Forgive a debt

(courtesy of the Random Acts of Kindness Foundation)

Pause to Ponder
- How can you be kind to yourself today?
- How has receiving a kindness affected your life?
- Contemplate a kindness that was especially significant.
- What random acts of kindness might you commit on your own? With some friends?
- Consider performing three anonymous acts of kindness each week. Record how this makes you feel.
- What changes within yourself do you notice?

Soul Sounds

The song we sing best is our own.

Sixteen-year-old Nikki Chooi sways ever so slightly. His adolescent self-consciousness dissipates as he transforms into an elegant extension of the music he makes. As he moves into the score, his body melds with the violin he holds, becoming a channel for the sounds that whisper one minute and charge full force the next. The intensity of the performance unleashes spontaneous tears from his audience who knows they are witnessing a mystical communion of body and spirit.

"Where are you when you play? What happens inside you?" I ask the young man after his audience releases him from their passionate applause. He smiles shyly, hesitates, and says, "I leave."

Ah, I think. The music is his pause, the magic that takes him from here to heaven. But when he "leaves" he transports those listening with him on his journey. Such is the power of music.

As with playing in a garden or reading a grand novel, music is the perfect, transcendent pause; it is the language of the universe and the soul food that kindles life's passion.

A Sousa march can mobilize a nation and *Auld Lang Syne* can prompt total strangers to warmly embrace when the New Year's bells ring. Whether we speak Dutch or Swahili, sounds that pierce the heart bridge this world with the next as we take a detour from the runaway world. "We live in the four corners of our minds," says Deborah Millar, a classical singer. "Music lets us bypass the intellect and go straight to the spirit, to the intuitive."

I shall always remember hearing the great cellist Yo-Yo Ma play at a concert I attended several years ago. Like young Nikki Chooi, Ma is a magician who can summon the angels with the touch of his bow. I had brought my daughter with me even though she was a tender tot of five. I'm glad I did. Something extraordinary happened that day. Ma is a consummate master, and that afternoon he seemed to channel a celestial presence. The large concert hall was absolutely quiet as he took us with him into an experience beyond human knowing. I glanced at my daughter and saw her sitting straight up on the edge of her seat, mesmerized. Like her, we all were captives at that moment, spellbound. Ma, too, had "left," taking us with him into a fleeting communion with his angels.

Music Makes Heaven Rock

Shivon Robinsong and Denis Donnelly direct the Gettin' Higher Choir, a non-audition choral group. Three hundred singers gather weekly to warble through African chants, gospel hymns, and show tunes. It is not a choir in the religious sense, but a gathering of people who simply want to sing. "We sing because we love it, not just to prepare for concerts (although we also do that)," says Shivon. "It is about expressing ourselves."

There are no auditions and no one is put on the spot,

says Jan, a choir member for the past two years, adding with a laugh, "Some of us read music; others just read the words." Like many in the group, Jan stumbled upon singing. "I was telling a friend that one day I want to join a choral group. She looked at me hard and said, 'Don't wait. Do it now.' When she explained that a close friend had just been diagnosed with a terminal illness, her message to me was clear."

"Anybody can sing," says Shivon. "Sadly, many of us are told that we can't and so we silence our song, our personal voice, and miss one of the greatest joys of being human. Finding our own voice is much more than determining if we are tenors or baritones. It is about discovering the songs deep inside us, about expressing who we are at the deepest level."

Shivon has observed that traditional cultures use singing to bind together their communities. "In our society, however, music has become largely commercial, oriented toward performance by the few for the many," she says. "The deeper promise of music for all has been forgotten."

Linda had hesitated to join a choir because of the daunting prospect of the audition process. Shivon's open-door, no-audition format removed that barrier. "Once the choir starts singing I forget any bad moments in the day. I lose myself to the music. And, although I am a shy person, I feel so welcome. All defenses drop away and I can be exactly who I am. It is a truly authentic act. Making music, being in harmony with others, is the ultimate expression of love. And that's what I feel when I sing."

Those Enchanting Evenings
There is no greater delight then a springtime rhapsody

of birdsong. The seemingly random chirps and trills create stunning arias of immense complexity. These unscripted occasions, like sunsets and sunrises, are unique to that instant in time. If we close our eyes, shut off the chatter in our heads, and allow the sounds to seep inside, the song gets even better, for that is when we hear the nuances of nature's lyrical conversation.

Instinctively, we know music affects our moods. Now, Penn State researchers Valerie N. Stratton, a psychologist, and Annette H. Zalonowski, a music specialist, have the data to back that up. They determined that music makes us feel more optimistic, joyful, friendly, and relaxed—be it rock and roll or a Brahms sonata. It takes us into a place that is ours alone, yet it can transcend and overcome that which divides us. It captures the pathos and the joy of the human experience and is the unseen force that can reduce a hardened soul to tears, create moments of sheer bliss, and unearth memories buried in the decades. When we sing our own song, we express who we are on an elemental level. It is a pause that can re-enchant our world.

Pause to Ponder

- What are your most memorable musical moments, the ones that moved you to bliss? To tears?
- When did you last take a silent walk and really listen to the sounds of nature?
- How does music influence your moods?
- What memories does a particular song evoke?
- Instead of using television as background sound, try switching to soft music. Notice how it affects the mood in your home.
- When could you create a musical pause in your day?

Retreats

Time away brings us home.

The rush of the city is miles away from this path that winds from the top of the road towards the sea. It takes Kena through stands of hemlock, cedar, and stately Sitka spruce. Beneath the trees, a tangle of moss and ferns shields an invisible universe of insects and small rodents. Deer, cougar, and black bears have walked the path where she now treads. In a clearing she sees a log cabin with branches hovering over its collapsing roof. Who lived here, or when, she does not know. But this remnant of recent human habitation is slowly vanishing beneath a confusion of brambles. Over time, it will disintegrate into the earth.

The air feels cooler as she continues along the path, a welcome relief from the midsummer heat. She brushes against a thicket of salal bushes with purple berries dangling beneath their sinewy stems, strips some off, and tosses the "poor man's blueberries" into her mouth. Later she will dry the leaves and, in the deep of winter, brew them for tea.

As she continues towards the shore, the forest's heady perfume mixes with the scent of sea. Suddenly the path opens to a deserted beach. The sand is littered with driftwood, broken clamshells, and clumps of seaweed left behind when the tide receded. Kena notices a weathered log and sits on it, watching *sandpipers scurry along the water's edge. Distant islands frame the scene in this vast theater for one.*

She is immersed in the wonder of this place—one not battered by the bite of power saws, the assault of backhoes, or the shattering shrill of leaf blowers. The land is as it should be: living and dying, bending not resisting, yet constant in its unfathomable splendor. Here she will pause. This place is her personal retreat, the place where she can contemplate nature's goodness.

Our detachment from the natural environment has become something of a cliché, yet the sad truth remains that more of us are making less and less time for even short pauses from the daily grind. We are losing our way in the whirl of busyness. And if a major crunch happens (a sudden illness, the death of a loved one, or job loss) we will have to face life's priorities head-on.

Pausing to retreat from our everyday life, if only for an afternoon, is an essential tool to balance a hurried life. It keeps us centered and sane.

Like a good hearty meal on a wintry night, solitude and contemplation feed our souls. They let us look closely at our lives, shake off the roles we play, abandon the masks we wear, and get real with ourselves. Whether we escape to a tent in the backyard or to a spiritual retreat center in the middle of nowhere, there is nothing like a one-on-one affair with nature to put our world back on its axis.

Stepping away from the runaway life, if only for short periods, affords us "thinking space." We can do it in any location that resonates with our innermost needs and encourages us to assess our lives and contemplate where we're going. It is a place just for *me*-time that will give our minds space to rest and open us to new possibilities.

Retreats are personal, tailor-made experiences. Like clearing our homes of clutter and distractions, going to a place apart from the one we know eliminates the triggers that turn our minds outward instead of inward. We are in charge as we choose the focus of the retreat, the length, and what we want to accomplish (which might be nothing at all).

While retreats are respites for the soul, they can also be rip-roaring adventures. Wilderness escapes in the mountains or in isolated cabins in the desert appeal to some. Rafting down raging rivers, hiking along mountain ridges, and backwoods camping also help us to know who we are and what matters most to us.

Places to hide away are as varied as the shells on Kena's beach. While some of us might prefer a day in a park or a weekend in the woods, retreat centers are growing in popularity. Some can be expensive, but many ask only for donations or have set modest rates.

Renée Lessard is a retreat junkie who likes the routines of Christian monasteries. "It depends how crazed I feel, but I have gone for just three days. Sometime I stay as long as eight," says the Los Angeles-based psychotherapist. "I like solitude and I like quiet. God's first language is silence. When I'm away I can listen and tap into who I am. The regimented schedule for prayer forces me to pause—to stop what I am doing and come to a place of silence."

She is a follower of Father Thomas Keating, a Cistercian monk who has headed St. Joseph's monastery in Spencer, Massachusetts, for three decades. Keating also founded the Centering Prayer movement that involves thirty minutes of meditation, twice a day.[4] "This might seem impossible when so many of us have lives that are so filled," he wrote, "but people who [practice Centering Prayer] tell me it changes their perspective. In their moments of contemplation, they discern that many of the things they were so busy doing are not necessary. They find their own reality." He has written several books in which he melds the Christian contemplative tradition with insights from contemporary psychology. His approach has struck a chord in North America where his following is growing.

Centering Prayer Is Simple to Perform:

• Choose a word as the symbol of your intention to consent to God's presence and His action within, such as: Father, Lord, Love, Peace, or Shalom
• Sit with your eyes closed and silently think of your word symbol; allow yourself to fill with God's presence
• If your mind wanders, return to your contemplative word
• When your prayer time is ended, remain still and silent for a couple of minutes as you gently re-enter the outside world

---

Many retreats are situated in stunning settings and some may be closer than you think. Queenswood Centre, operated by the Sisters of St. Ann on a secluded estate along the oceanside, is within walking distance of my home. This contemplative sanctuary is very affordable and welcomes men and women of all faiths. Those who go there can stay for a few hours or participate in longer, organized programs. As with many similar centers, Queenswood offers guided and unguided experiences during which participants walk or read, arrange for spiritual counseling, or just sit in the gardens. With a little research, you may find somewhere for quiet contemplation close to where you live.

Stories abound of those who made abrupt and dramatic changes in how they live after suffering through life-threatening illnesses or ego-busting traumas. In most cases, those changes are soulful and permanent. Lucinda Vardey, once a hotshot literary agent, had one such experience after surviving a serious illness. She left her high-powered life to embrace a more contemplative one that led her to establish Migliara, a spiritual retreat in a restored 500-year-old farmhouse. Located in the sun-drenched beauty of Tuscany, Lucinda describes the retreat as "a home for souls, a place to restore and guide. All who come to Migliara leave with greater peace, clearer vision, and a nourished soul." Lucinda's spiritual interest bridges the teachings of east and west and the programs she offers include treks in the footsteps of St. Francis and a pilgrimage to explore the lives and lessons of Italian holy women.

Trusting her instincts led my friend Lynn, a harried teacher, to a center in California's Sierra Mountains. "I needed to get away. Life was piling up on me and I knew it was the right thing for me to do. The experience was phenomenal. I lived for a week in a cooperative, respectful environment that put me right in the middle of nature. I learned that life is like climbing a mountain: it is so much easier to do if we lighten our inner load. I also learned that it is okay to be spiritual, to dance in the wind, and to feel free and happy."

I believe we each have a special place that speaks to the very marrow in our bones. Going to such a place is a worthy pilgrimage. Whether it is a corner in our garden or a trip to Migliara, pausing for quiet and contemplation in a beautiful natural setting brings us back to ourselves.

"I need to take an emotional breath, step back, and remind myself who's actually in charge of my life," says author Judith M. Knowlton. How right she is. Retreats give us what our soul seeks. Whether it be for adventure, meditative time, relationship-building with friends or our partner, or to spend time with our God, a pause from our daily distractions is an emotional tonic that lets us go deep inside, resolve issues, and celebrate life: a powerful, prayerful pause.

Creating Your Getaway

As with planning a vacation, questions arise when we go to a retreat:

- *Can I spare the time?* Of course you can! Pausing to give ourselves this gift of time will leave us with energy and insight to address the challenges we face before they send us scrambling for cover. We might be worried, tired, struggling with a family or relationship conflict, contemplating a career change, or approaching a major life passage. Many centers offer spiritual and life counseling.
- *What about cost?* Many spiritual centers have surprisingly affordable arrangements. The location, length of your stay, level of facilities, and whether the center you choose is commercial or non-profit, will determine the cost. Look for recommendations from churches or religious orders in your area. You might also research the Internet for monastic retreats, adventure retreats, spa retreats, or youth retreats.
- *Where should I go?* What type of environment do you need at this time? Close to home or new surroundings? Contemplate the environment that speaks to you. When

your wishes, thoughts, and mindset are clear, watch how the perfect place finds its way into your life.

- *Before you go.* Be definite about your purpose. Know what you want to achieve and how you want to spend your time. Writing down what you want to gain from the experience, as well as the questions you need answered, will help clarify your goals.
- *What to take.* Bring a journal, books that inspire you, art material if you want to draw or paint, walking shoes, and a couple of changes of quick-dry, wrinkle-free clothes. Packing light leaves your mind free. Ask ahead what physical activities are available and bring what you need to participate. For light-packing tips, read "The Essential Traveler," a chapter in my book *Unclutter Your Life: Transforming Your Physical, Mental, and Emotional Space.*

Retreat Centers Mentioned Above:

St. Joseph's Abbey – *www.spencerabbey.org*
167 North Spencer Rd., Spencer, MA 0552-1233
Telephone: (508) 885-8710

Migliara Retreats – *www.dallaluce.com*
46 Berryman St., Toronto, ON M5R 1M6
Telephone: (416) 323-1133

Queenswood Centre –*www.queenswoodcentre.com*
2494 Arbutus Rd., Victoria, BC V8N 1V8
Telephone: (250) 477-3822

Pause to Ponder
- If you have never been to a retreat, ask around for people who have. What was their experience and how did it affect their life?
- When, if ever, have you taken time away by yourself, just for yourself?
- What do you envision as your ideal retreat experience?
- If you spoke to God face-to-face, what would you say?
- If you could ask God just one question, what would it be?

Past Connections

The roots of a tree feed even the smallest leaf.

A *fascination with yesterday is catching on. Television shows and books are enticing us to scour through second-hand shops and rummage through steamer trunks. Dusty old junk now just might be a treasure!*

If we pause and think awhile, we might also find a glimpse of ourselves woven into handmade quilts and fading diaries. Do they turn us into hopeless romantics taunted by the mystique of yesterday? Are we fascinated with delicate Depression glass or well-used walking sticks? What about our interest in old war medals or silver snuff boxes? Things from the past can feed a curiosity about those who used them—especially if they belonged to someone from a branch of our family tree.

Contemplating our personal past lets us play detective as we roam through a time when life moved at a more human pace. Stepping into those gentler times is a potent remedy to tame today's rushed world.

An appreciation of our ancestry can be a delightful past-pause and a refreshing, grounding detour from the present.

Pausing to consider how our ancestral past influences our life today can give us glimpses into who, and what, came before us. Although former generations had their share of challenges, just thinking of an era of elegant manners, afternoon tea, or mint juleps on a shaded verandah gives us a mental reprieve from the realities of rush-hour traffic, cellphones, and e-mail.

Marion moves with grace through her home, in which she keeps a collection of porcelain tea services. Some date back to 1810 and include pieces brought from Japan by her great-grandmother. When I asked about them she replied, "I remember my grandmother using them to serve tea. Those little cups are a special connection to her." Her voice softened as she imagined the craftsman hand-grinding the pigments and painting each cup before setting them in the kiln. "Such skill and care shows they must have been made with great affection."

Bonnie is also captivated by remnants of yesterday. She has a love of flower-patterned china, tiny thimbles, and exotic shawls with silk fringes, and she is fascinated with hand-painted cookie jars. She likes to muse about the grand occasions when wearing rhinestone earrings and white kid gloves was the rage. As we chatted, she turned to a tablecloth decorated with detailed needlework. "This was likely made in the 1920s for a wedding gift. There are countless hours of work in this lovely piece. I feel as if I'm holding history in my hands," she said as she ran her fingers lightly over the surface. "Things like this deserve to be appreciated—to be loved, especially if they were made by someone in the family."

While charming tablecloths and old china may have intriguing stories to tell us, so do the people who belong to our personal past. Having something of theirs, if only a flower vase or an old pipe, connects us to them, as does learning about who they were and how they lived. Knowing about our ancestors gives us clues about ourselves. We might recognize our distinctive nose in an aged sepia family photograph, but do we know from whom we inherited a penchant for mathematics, a rebellious spirit, a talent for politics, or a love of music? Looking back, if only a generation or two, gives us a sense of who *we* are, and it can be a very pleasant and insightful pause.

What About Aunt Sophie?

Sherry Irvine, a recognized genealogist and author of several books on British ancestry, has some thoughts on how learning about the people in our past can affect us. "We live busy lives and often we are not as well-anchored as people of previous generations. Knowing our family history gives us roots, a sense of place. In researching our family history, we can establish a link in the continuum of time. It takes us off the fast track."

What began as a hobby while her children were young is now an exciting career that takes her around the world. "Two things sparked my interest in my ancestry," says Sherry. "The vast amount of information and fascinating stories the older people told about my father's family contrasted with my mother's great reticence to talk about her past. When I was fifteen, I learned she had been married before. That was quite a surprise and left me with a lingering curiosity to find out more."

Genealogy 101

- Speak to older family members about the past and record the stories
- Record the names and details of people in family photographs
- Always verify the facts. Memories can be faulty. Confirm all information
- Noting the source of your facts as they are gathered saves time and trouble later
- If using the Internet for your search, organize your favorite sites
- Talk to people experienced in genealogy. Take a course, often offered at community centers

(courtesy of Sherry Irvine)

I was reminded of the power, and pleasures, of relishing our ancestry when garlic farmer Pat Zanichelli descended on a late-summer party, bearing trays of that season's harvest, roasted and ready to enjoy. We went wild. The pungent tapas that we love today were a hit with Egypt's pyramid-building slaves as well, and the pièce de résistance of feasts for Roman troops. Garlic's power to heal, fend off unwanted advances, and repel bothersome vampires is legendary. Pat has a pure passion for these alluring alliums.

"My affection for garlic comes from my Italian heritage," he says. "Growing and eating garlic is like breathing, a part of life." He looked across his garlic fields and murmured, "It's too beautiful for words. I measure time by the planting, nurturing, and harvesting of each crop."

Pat's family was living in Regina when his mother died. He and his siblings were sent to live with Italian friends. "Like us, this family followed the old country's traditions," he remembers. "They give me a sense of where I came from."

As I selected a succulent morsel from the fast-emptying tray, I considered how Pat's life had a rhythm that has flowed through his family for generations.

Pat's Sautéed Garlic Cloves
Garlic cloves—one for each person

Boil peeled garlic cloves for 2 to 3 minutes. Drain and rinse in cold water.

Melt sufficient butter to cook garlic gently for 15 to 18 minutes, tossing frequently. When cooled, mash cloves to spread on focaccia bread, use in sauces, or toss whole into pasta, rice, or seafood dishes.

I occasionally wander through an auction house close to my home and contemplate the stories that the rows of pictures, boxes of old cards, and fancy silverware might tell. We will never know them, for when the auctioneer's gavel comes down, they will be lost forever. The time to ask questions and hear those stories is now.

Setting aside time to chat with senior members of our family can be great fun and the perfect Sunday afternoon pause. They had a world without cyber-saturation, one where people wrote letters *by hand*, fixed what broke, and took time to chinwag over the back fence. Perhaps Great-Aunt Sophie might relate how Uncle Ted made the old cabinet in the corner when he returned from the war, or how she crocheted the good tablecloth during the journey from Ireland. These little bits of the past inform our own lives with a richer understanding of the people with whom we share an ancestral bond.

Have we shared stories about *our* special things or the heirlooms we have inherited? Do our children know the names of the people in the family photographs? Have they been told who made the christening dress that has been handed down through the generations? Do they know that the hand-written poem that hung on Grandma's bedroom wall was written by her father, or that the good china she used for Sunday dinner had belonged to her grandmother? Taking time to share the stories of our special items ensures our personal and family histories survive, and writing them down is even better.

The power of possessions lies in what they represent and the memories they evoke. Christmas ornaments handed down through the generations, a wedding ring, or family photos can evoke memories of childhood celebrations. A set of napkin rings or Aunt Sophie's silverware might remind us of special family dinners, the time when Uncle Harry came to visit, or the day we graduated from college.

Pausing to think about those who came before us enriches our sense of who we are. It opens us to the immense pleasures of momentarily putting life in reverse—of touching, if only vicariously, a world where people came first, and time together mattered more than time at the office.

Paper-thin teacups, decades-old tablecloths, and home-grown garlic can invite us into a time before our own and unite the generations with the durable bond of our family's unique history.

Pause to Ponder
- What memories or events from the past play a role in your life today?
- What do you know about your family tree?
- Do some of your preferences and dislikes mirror those of an ancestor?
- When did you last talk about your family history with an elderly relative?
- What questions would you like answered?
- Have you made an up-to-date inventory of your special possessions?
- Have you written down the stories associated with them?
- To research family ancestry, please consult the Reading List for books on genealogy.

Everyday Pauses ...

keep life in balance

Putting the brakes on a runaway life means living fully, every minute. Rather than wait for the weekend, we create pauses every day to cook a great meal, take a nap, buff our brains and our bodies, too. Everyday pauses are self-nurturing habits that sustain and enhance life. By delighting in our family, sleeping deeply, caring for others, setting limits, and acknowledging we are meant to dance and dream and play, we will help ensure our world turns a little slower and more softly.

Burnout or Balance?

Do the things that rock your socks.

"*My carpenter schedules his work around moose-hunting season,*" *quips my friend Russell when I ask about his house renovations. The former urbanite, who moved with his wife to a small coastal community, was remarking on how the folks in his new neighborhood determine their priorities. Building Russell's back porch was no match for hunting moose.*

Similarly I was stunned to watch a food vendor in a southern French hamlet close up shop as I approached him, money in hand, on a scorching July day. It was just after noon and he said he was off to lunch (to be followed, I suspected, by a snooze). He'd return mid-afternoon. I could come back then. Imagine someone in downtown Toronto, London, or New York telling a client to come back after lunch, or when hunting season is over!

Unlike the folks described above, many of us tend to pack more, not less, into our days. Being busy and *being seen to be busy* are the hallmarks of our performance-driven culture. It is how we define ourselves. Too often, we allow our many commitments and others' demands on our time to distract us from what we really want to be doing—whether that is stalking wild game or spending time with our family.

Time Thieves and Monkey Business

A woman I shall call Clare loves to entertain. I have watched her whip up dinner for six after putting in a full day at work. Between the time she leaves work and the time her guests arrive, she will squeeze in a workout at the gym and do a quick pick-up around the house. Trouble is, she often leaves her company in mid-bite. "She's had a full week," apologized her husband during our first visit to their home when she fell asleep between the main course and dessert. "She simply runs out of steam."

While much is written about the effects of today's frenzied lifestyle on our mental and physical health, the issue is most powerfully conveyed in the 1992 film *Baraka*. Masterminded by filmmaker Ron Fricke, it is a wondrous, compelling collage of images and music, throughout which we experience silence and solitude, heart-breaking destruction, chaotic activity, and stunning landscapes; and it shoves our obsession with busyness in our faces.

The film opens with what I call the "ultimate pause." The camera slowly pans over mountains in an isolated region of Japan before focusing on a hot spring hidden among the crevices. Lounging alone in the steaming mist, a snow monkey gazes into the clear night sky. He appears to be on an inner journey of delight, as if experiencing a moment of bliss. The scene is powerful in its simple eloquence, a riveting vision of deep contentment. Oh, to be that monkey. He (or was it a she?) had it all—perfect peace in a setting of arresting beauty.

Pausing to consider what really matters to us is worth

every minute we give it. Are we living a life that lifts us out of bed in the morning to eagerly greet the day? Do we happily anticipate tomorrow? Are we using our talents, learning something new each day, and having fun? Or are we living "on autopilot" where one day dissolves into the next?

Our current culture is consumed by an anxiety about status that is fueled by expectations which stretch us to capacity. It praises the company executive who puts in seventy-hour weeks and admires the student who makes the honor roll in school, performs in the school band, belongs to the soccer team, and sings in the church choir. When summer vacation rolls around, she marches off to drama camp to get a head start on next year's auditions for the school play—all the better to prepare her for seventy-hour work weeks when she hits the big time like her dad. (A Canadian study[5] showed that nearly half of respondents cut back on sleep to pack more activities into their day.[6])

Even those who retire cannot escape. "I'm as active as ever," says Sharon, a recent retiree. "I don't know when I found time to work!" She admits to getting caught up in a whirlwind of commitments that left her little time for herself. "I was out all the time. It got crazy. Now I block a day a week at home. While that might not seem like a big deal, to me it is a huge step in taking back my time."

I hear much the same from others who have replaced the demands of the workplace with bridge games, lunches with friends, volunteering at the church, golf, painting class, or courses on Impressionist art, creative writing, and computer literacy—all in the same week! "It's sad but it seems our worth is judged by what we do," says Sharon. "Being busy means you're still in the game." Sharon also speaks of the pressure to put others first. "I think for most women it feels unnatural and somehow wrong to think about what's good for *me,* so we overload our lives taking care of others."

Asserting the right to decide how we use our time is the most profound choice we can make. Finance wizard Suze Orman says we too often confuse *who we are* with *what we have.* Somehow we have been sold on the idea that bigger and better is best, and when we achieve that, up goes the bar and we start over again. As our anxiety level spirals upward, our contentment quotient plummets and our leisure time disappears. We have confused happiness with the buzz of instant gratification, yet studies confirm we are less content than we were in the lean days before World War II.

If only we could set boundaries and find a balance that respects our human, rather than superhuman, nature. Yet, we are pressured to work our tails off, jamming the rafters of our homes with stuff we do not need. As a society, we have never had so many choices, and we have never been so over-worked, over-stressed, and over-tired.

We are unlikely to have a secluded mountain hideaway nearby, and the pressures of real life could overshadow bliss in the twilight. We may feel we have little choice about what we do, citing such barriers as obligations to others lack of time, money, or opportunity. It comes back to priorities. It might be that raising young children, caring for ageing or ill family members, fueling a career, or topping up the bank account are what matters, now. But we can take small steps towards a life that is in harmony with our inner rhythm. We can make choices that respect our responsibilities to others and honor ourselves. But first we have to dismiss the time thieves, set boundaries, and embrace the thrill of taking charge.

About Balance

Oh, to live a passionate, vibrant life—one that makes our socks rock. More of us are coming to recognize that life is a series of moments, one flowing into the next, and that we are often responsible for how those moments unfold. We are realizing that life's biggest payback—happiness—arrives in truckloads when we love what we do. It is a delicate dance, an elegant balance of self and others.

The gurus of balanced living suggest that we allocate time for work, family, community, health, and faith; I suggest balance is really about making the things that feed our inner fire a priority in our lives. Balance is about choosing passionate living over a pedestrian existence. That could mean working with the poor, developing safer industrial practices, lobbying for political changes, dazzling the world with artistic gifts, or being the cheeriest and most efficient restaurant server in the business. Balance is about giving time and energy to live our personal truth, our authentic life, but this often means taking a detour from the runaway life—sometimes for a little while, sometimes forever.

Writer Michelle Greysen shares her story:

"The people I know who live in the bush laugh at us city folks who live like lunatics all year long just so we can afford to go to our cottages or take the tent camping and live like them for two weeks each year. I took this yearning to the extreme and have totally changed my lifestyle. I gave up a six-figure income because everything I accomplished was not in line with what I felt I was *meant* to be accomplishing. So, I sold my 4,000-square-foot home with the best of everything in it, edited out much of the stuff in my life, and kept only what I dearly loved. I left the work world and opted to be a writer in a small town where I didn't know anyone.

"The financial gains from the big house meant I now had no bills and no need for a day job, no harried commute, and no office hassles. I also have no fancy granite countertops or top-of-the-line appliances. Gone, too, are the nine sinks and five toilets I don't have to clean. Life is now about who I *am*, not what I *do*. I enjoy myself more, laugh more, and sleep better. And I have that get-away-feeling every day. I know I am not alone in 'shoving it all for a simple lifestyle' (I still love my good scotch and big velour bath sheets, I just don't need a cupboardful anymore), but it feels like I have discovered a great big secret—I feel like I'm on a holiday every day."

Michelle's story brings me back to the French countryside. While those who live there may have the jump on midday siestas and crafting great cheese, they also understand balance and boundaries. As writer Joe Sornberger wrote when he returned from his travels there, "I learned that eating small portions of slowly prepared food is better than consuming big meals of fast food. Conversations are better than meetings. Making money is certainly important, but making the most of the moment is, ultimately, more important."

Balance, it seems, is not a question of managing time, but of making choices that resonate with who we really are. It means recognizing that, while we just might be able to do it all, we cannot do it all at the same time. It means setting very personal priorities aligned with our unique self, not those imposed by a culture or society that thrives on frantic competition and artificial standards of cool. Ultimately, setting priorities and maintaining balance is about knowing and managing yourself, like that little snow monkey in the film and Russell's carpenter. After all, it is your life.

Tips to Take Charge of Your Life

- Choose three goals you want to accomplish. Write these out and post them where you will see them every day. (Until they are in writing, they are not goals, just dreams)
- Make a daily written plan that respects your energy level and interests. Include time for one of your goals. Make your dream activity a top priority
- Commit to doing fewer things, but give more time to what gives your life a happy jolt
- Plan to arrive at appointments a few minutes early. This allows for traffic and parking delays
- Delegate or share responsibility for routine activities. Encourage family members to clean their own rooms, make their lunches, do their own laundry, and be responsible for at least one household chore
- What are the high-maintenance elements in your life? How can these be simplified or perhaps eliminated?
- How difficult is your home to maintain? Can you reduce, share, or hire outside help for some household chores?
- Eliminate social or volunteer activities that have become too demanding
- Isolate your time-wasters. Say no to trivial activities that will not bring value to your life
- Block off time that is just for you. Make this time non-negotiable
- Put enjoyable activities at the top of your list
- Phone calls eat up time. Schedule these when it is convenient for you

- Divide your time into manageable chunks. Forget multi-tasking and plan enough time to complete what you start
- Keep a two-week log of the time you spend watching TV

Pause to Ponder
- What do you really want to be doing with your life now? In five years?
- What is one activity you would spend more time doing if you could?
- Before you agree to take on a new commitment, ask about the time requirement.
- How will this commitment affect you and your family?
- Plan today what you want to do tomorrow.
- Look out for a screening of *Baraka* (or try to get the video).

Silent Treatment

Imagine hearing the wind speak.
That's what real quiet is —
when the slightest sound can travel forever.

He sits in a quiet garden. His stillness blends with the landscape and soon he is drawn into the silence. At first he hears nothing, and then, as if an unseen conductor had lifted a baton, he detects the rustle of leaves on the branches above him. The more he listens, the more complex the sounds become. Now a wind chime tinkles, adding grace notes to the melody of a purple finch that is warbling to its mate. A robin stakes its territory with a telltale carol of "cheer-up, cheer-up, cheer-up." A crackle in the undergrowth betrays a squirrel rummaging about. Over on a pond, newly hatched ducklings cheep as they dart through lily pads chasing flies. Never again will this impromptu concert, this natural symphony, unfold exactly as it has now. It is an inimitable interlude of sound.

If only we could bottle those exquisite moments of loveliness! But we live in a bewildering din of babble. From honking horns to ringing cellphones, noise defines us as a culture that rattles and rolls. It plays havoc with our innards and shatters our serenity. We need quiet time, lots of it, daily. Silence, that ephemeral quality that re-engages our senses, is God's soul food. It's the pause that feeds the spirit.

A few years ago, Victoria, where I live, had an opportunity to experience life as it might have been before cars clogged our roads and traffic noise became inescapable. Winters here are usually so mild that it rarely snows. That season, much to our delight, down came the white stuff and children dashed outside to play before it started to melt. There was no need to panic. The sky dumped buckets for three solid days and nights, turning the city into a wonderland of white. In a city without snow-removal equipment, this caused more than a minor stir. Roads shut down and the airports closed. Even the ferries connecting us to the outside world sat tied to the docks looking like huge vanilla ice cream cones. What might have been a disaster, turned out to be a gift.

As gardens and boulevards transformed from lush winter green into pristine landscapes of white, kids hauled toboggans out of storage, snowmen (and snowwomen) emerged from the drifts, and kindness flowed as easily as the snow had fallen. Neighbors who before might have offered each other merely a curt hello, now checked to see if all was well. Impromptu gatherings replaced planned get-togethers. We had no choice but to pause.

For the first time in my life I experienced a city as it might have been prior to the cacophony that followed the inventions of Henry Ford. All was so still that we heard snow fall from tree branches and crunch under our feet. It was delightful. It was then I understood just how tiring and mind-numbing is the racket we live with and how it incites an adrenaline rush that goads us into a higher gear.

I realized that a period of silence each day is as essential to well-being as food and water.

Noise Hurts

The bustle of a busy metropolis was energizing for Jeremy, who had moved from a mid-sized city to live and work in the action-packed center of London, England. Central London's non-stop activity makes it one of the planet's most energetic places. It was a grand experience. Within a few blocks of his flat, he could absorb the excitement of Piccadilly Circus, stroll through Regent Street, or catch the crowds milling about the theater district. After three years of living there, however, Jeremy has these observations: "I went through a honeymoon phase at first. I liked the charged atmosphere with all the action, the cars, and people-noise. After awhile, I started to filter it out, something that happens naturally. Yet, now the noise has made its way back into my consciousness and it affects me physically and mentally. I've decided to move. Living in London is simply overwhelming."

In his practice as a doctor of traditional Chinese medicine, Jeremy sees symptoms of prolonged physical and mental distress that he attributes to our quickening pace of life. "We lose our appetites, relying on fast food and short-term stimulants such as sugary foods and caffeine," he says. "When we are stressed, our breathing becomes shallow, creating less oxygen in our systems. Our adrenal glands, which pump out hormones to deal with stress, become overtaxed. This induces fatigue. If we stay wound-up over the long term, they burn out."

He also added that our rushed lives cause us to live in our heads. Noisy environments contribute to this state he calls "busy mind" by acting as a barrier between our heads and our hearts. Background noise keeps us off guard and unable to focus, grinding down our senses.

A study shows more than two-thirds of British households are experiencing nighttime noise levels higher than international health guidelines recommend. Investigators determined that men exposed to high levels of environmental noise had a 50 percent greater risk of heart attack than did those in the reference group where the sound was less than 60 decibels. Women subjected to high environmental sound levels have more than triple the risk.[7]

The Quiet Revolution

Shh, a quiet revolution is underway and it can be heard worldwide. Noise, that pervasive distraction that we may feel powerless to control, is not an inevitable fact of life. We have a right to speak up and demand a quieter, kinder society—one that does not impose its will, but respects a gentler way of life.

A small, but effective, advocacy group wants to press the mute button on our increasingly raucous society. They believe we have a "right to quiet" and they are not waiting for the next big snowstorm to talk about it. The Right to Quiet Society wants us to join the new "silent majority" by pausing now to decrease the noise in our communities.[8] Whether petitioning city councils to ban leaf blowers and other noise-inducing monsters, maintaining an informational website, distributing newsletters and talking (quietly) about the effects of noise on our health and quality of life, the society is raising awareness and creating change.

These determined change-makers feel much of the

racket we live with is tolerated only because we do not really understand the effects noise has on us. While the group acknowledges a noiseless society is impossible, it adamantly believes in taking action to quiet life down.

Goals of the Right to Quiet Society

- Stricter regulation of aircraft flights over populated areas and national parks
- Enforcement of laws governing unmuffled vehicles, especially "chopper" motorcycles
- Regulation of noise-producing watercraft, especially personal watercraft
- Ban on leaf blowers, or at least a drastic reduction in permitted dates and hours of use
- Reductions in the permitted hours of power gardening (lawn mowers, trimmers)
- Regulation of maximum noise levels of sirens, and reduction in volume when used by night
- Regulation of maximum noise levels of [vehicle] backup beepers, with sensible rules about what vehicles should have them
- Ban on personal amplified radio and music in most public spaces, beginning with the declaration of more parks and beaches as quiet zones
- Voluntary reduction in the amount of program audio piped into private establishments such as restaurants, malls, and doctors' and dentists' offices
- Recognition of the right to quiet in the workplace
- Recognition of noise as cruelty to animals (in feedlots, on farms, in pet stores, or homes where loud music is constantly played)

• Provide telephone callers with the option to hear silence while on hold [instead of Muzak and other programming]

(courtesy of the Right to Quiet Society)

For those of us who negotiate life in a non-stop work-world, a quiet refuge may be closer than we think. Philip Roderick, an English priest and an advocate for more serene communities, recognized the need for daily interludes of quiet and began a project that has come to be known as the Quiet Garden Trust. These places, he suggested, would provide relief for city workers and serve as places for contemplation and repose—mini-escapes for spiritual refreshment in a natural setting. Roderick's idea led to the first designated Quiet Garden in 1992 at Stoke Park Farm in Stoke Poges, Buckinghamshire. Fittingly, the farm is near the church of St. Giles where Thomas Gray wrote the famous *Elegy Written in a Country Churchyard*. Now, the Quiet Garden Trust has more than 260 registered properties in cities throughout eighteen countries including Canada, Australia, England, and the United States.[9] The demand for quiet places continues to grow and communities are responding. Montreal has a quiet garden at the Church of St. Andrew & St. Paul. The garden at St. Joseph's church near the Barbican in the heart of the City of London was once a small paved triangle surrounded on two sides by an iron fence. Trinity Square is a wonderful quiet space plunked in the middle of a quadrangle of Toronto skyscrapers where downtown workers can escape cellphones and e-mail to walk the labyrinth or take a few moments for reflection.

But quiet is not just about solitude. In New York, artist Paul Rebhan and musician Tony Noe went looking for a place to have a drink and talk. Good luck! Every bar they tried vibrated with grind-in-your-ear-while-I-grind-in-your-groin chaos. Frustrated with this, they concocted the idea of a "quiet party" where guests would talk softly (or pass notes, instead). They convinced the owner of the Scotch Bonnet, a midtown lounge in Manhattan, to hold the event. Nearly two hundred people silently crammed the bar. Music, cellphones, and other electronic devices were *verboten*. The party was a hit. People enjoyed the relaxed, no-stress ambience. Quiet parties are now being held around North America. A group has even started up in Beijing, one of the world's noisiest cities. Here's how an invitation to one of their gatherings explains the concept:

"A Quiet Party is a reaction against the typical bar scene where loud noise predominates and conversation is almost impossible without practically shouting at each other. It is also a new and innovative way to meet people and start new relationships. One section of the bar is designated for quiet conversation with quiet background music. The other part is the Quiet Zone where NO conversation is allowed at all! All communication is done by writing notes (using paper/pencils provided by the organizer). Sound strange? Perhaps...but people quickly get used to it, and find it both fun and liberating. It is reminiscent of passing notes in school and strangely similar to chatting with people on-line. People who come to a Quiet Party tend to experience the same phenomenon, and 'speak' more easily and freely—even with strangers—than they would normally. It also provides other forms of entertainment, such as poetry contests where we provide the first line of a poem and you finish it (funniest poem wins a prize), and chain stories where a pad of paper is passed from person to person, each adding to the story."

London's Heathrow Express, the commuter train running from the city center to the airport, has designated "quiet cars" where people are encouraged to speak softly and the use of cellphones is banned. The residents of Vancouver's West Side have successfully lobbied city council for a ban on leaf blowers; violators can expect a hefty fine of up to $2,000. The French government has instituted a policy that allows theater and concert hall owners to install cellphone-jamming equipment to stop all but emergency calls. Consumers have demanded silent household appliances and Miele, a German company, has risen to the challenge with a compact, super-quiet vacuum cleaner. Families are designating "quiet time" and "quiet zones" without phones, radios, or televisions in their homes. Some activists are demanding a workplace ban on unnecessary noise.

Tips to Create a Personal Quiet Zone

- Reduce second-hand noise in your home by putting the TV in a room with a door. Turn off the TV when it is not in use
- Reduce radio chatter by tuning into music stations. Keep the volume low
- Designate quiet time without radio or TV
- Oil hinges and put felt buffers on cupboard doors
- Put telephone ringers on low
- Start a quiet trend by using a push-reel or electric lawn mower. You'll get some exercise and your neighbours will thank you
- When it's time to replace your appliances, consider low-noise options
- When at home (and elsewhere if possible), turn off your cellphone ringer
- Choose quiet toys for your children

When we take on the task of reducing noise in our homes and the places in which we work, we can move through our days more easily and purposefully. We will sleep better and feel less rushed. Pausing to put a little quiet into our lives gives us an earful of serenity, a peaceful interlude. It muffles our mind-chatter, reduces mental clutter, and clears our interior space. When we create or seek out quiet and serene environments, we become more attuned to the lovely sounds around us. Giving ourselves this silent treatment every day helps us remember that, like taking an afternoon to do nothing at all, a little silence is good for the body and for the soul.

Pause to Ponder
- How does noise affect you?
- What everyday sounds in your day life irritate or soothe your soul?
- How can you soften or eliminate negative sounds?
- How might you create a quiet zone at home or work?
- Consider a silent weekend. If you do not live alone, you may want to spend the time at a place that offers silent retreats. A quick Internet search under "silent retreats" will bring up several options.
- Locate a quiet natural setting, perhaps a garden, to retreat from your daily routine.
- The last Wednesday in April is the annual International Noise Awareness Day, sponsored by the League for the Hard of Hearing (*www.lhh.org*). Why not be part of the "silent majority" and promote the day in your community?
- Visit the Right to Quiet Society website for research and thoughts on quiet living (*www.quiet.org*).

Family Matters

A good family sweetens life like nothing else can.

"What a disarming, mind-awakening marvel this first grandchild experience is," says proud grandpa, Steve MacDowall. "Now, I have to tell you, I was prepared. The way some people act with newborns is downright silly and I was determined to converse with her in a mature manner right from the beginning. There was no way I was going to inflict funny faces, unintelligible squeaky noises, and a bunch of gibberish when interacting with my grandchild. I researched a host of children's rhymes and songs that I felt would be appropriate to entertain and soothe her. So, I'm ready... they place the little bundle in my arms. Wow, so light, so small, so beautiful. Her eyes focus on me and she grabs my finger—she actually squeezes it. I walk away from everyone so I can talk to my new little buddy. I open my mouth and all that comes out is...gibberish, gobbledygook."

The birth of a baby is certainly cause for a celebration. What a wonder to behold the perfection of those sweet bundles of innocence...so untouched by the world and filled with potential! New life reminds us of the mystery of existence and the significance of family. It reminds us that our time on this planet is brief, but if we can find our talent, develop it, and then take it into the world to serve others, we will have made the journey worthwhile. We cannot do it alone, though. That is where family, however we choose to define it, comes in.

The healthy family is a powerful institution that transmits values and attitudes from one generation to the next. It offers a safe place to be spontaneous and unguarded. It holds the hands of those departing and whoops for joy when new members are born. At its best, family encourages independence, supports its members when times get rough, accepts differences, celebrates successes, is fiercely loyal (although there are times they might fight like heck, they stay a team), does not belittle or betray, and is a haven during these increasingly uncertain times. It is where we can wallow in the warmth of acceptance even if we occasionally go astray.

Families give us balance, a sense of grounding. They keep us centered in a constantly shifting world. Friends may move out of our lives for many reasons. Our professional or work culture may change. We might relocate, divorce, or remarry. New interests take us in new directions. Whatever happens "out there," however, our family is constant. For this reason, it is worth treasuring and safeguarding. Making time for our family—pausing for family—is as much for us, as it is for the others who join us for Thanksgiving dinner.

Preserving and protecting our "family space," be it spending time with our birth family or with the one we create, is as essential as food and water. When our physical needs are satisfied, it is our emotional and spiritual needs that ask for nourishment and this is what family is for.

I was impressed to hear the president of a large university give a speech in which she shared her life priorities; her family topped the list. Throughout her work week she makes time—pauses—for the special people in her life. She and her husband run with their dog most mornings. Her commitments are scheduled around birthdays and special occasions. When she is not attending a professional function, she is home for supper. "We kick right back," she says. "Even if it's macaroni and cheese, we sit at the table and light the candles. There are no distractions. No TV. No radio." The time she spends with her family significantly surpasses the American national average of 38.5 minutes a week.[11]

Childhood Is Not a Command Performance

Although the importance of family time is a high-profile issue, the facts tell a less happy story, especially when it comes to the little ones. Pressure to develop the next superstar is overshadowing the less glamorous task of raising happy, productive children. The demand to excel is wearing down the kids and burning out the parents. Parenting is now a competitive sport. Moms and dads (and grandparents) are making their kids their job as they dart between extra tutoring sessions, music lessons, gymnastics, and soccer practice. Classroom performance is tightly monitored. Teachers are screened and less-than-stellar results are cause for full-scale summit meetings. The pressure is intensifying as the standards rise.

We are panting through life, dragging our kids along with us. We seem to have forgotten that childhood is the time to play at life. It is a time *just for fun* before the very real demands of college, marriage, and mortgages.

I recall a conversation with Olympic soccer coach Bruce

Twamley, then a recently retired player. We were discussing my son, who was five years old and had shown an interest in the game. "Let him play for the heck of it," he said. "If he's got a burning need to play pro one day, he'll let *you* know." Bruce's comments mirror those of many former professionals who are not the ones hustling their kids off to 6 a.m. practices. Perhaps they know that, with millions of children playing organized sports in North America (for example, 550,000 Canadian kids play organized minor hockey in 3,200 arenas across the country), the chances to snag a professional contract are slim. If a child does, then what? The pros know it is a demanding, uncertain life with challenges that can eclipse the most lucrative salary contract if the personal foundations are not strong.

Secrets of a Successful Family
- Eat together
- Exercise together
- Play together
- Pause together
- Put families first

Let's pause and put families first. Leanne and Philip, parents of three young children, made a conscious decision to do just that. They live on a hobby farm where everyone pitches in to raise chickens and tend a market garden. The children also care for a pet goat, two dogs, rabbits, guinea pigs, turtles, and fish. Philip is a full-time, stay-at-home-dad while Leanne supports the family with her position as the director of a large non-profit agency. Dinner-hour dance classes and early morning hockey practices are not on their agenda. "We only raise kids once," says Leanne. "So *we* want time with them. That's our priority."

She told me that on Friday nights they make home-made pizza and popcorn and then watch a show. "The kids really look forward to this because they don't have TV during the week. On Saturdays, they clean the pet cages and their rooms. Then it is Games Night. It's really fun."

The children have a limit of two activities, one of which Leanne or Philip does with them. "Our son Noël wanted to learn horseback riding and so I take lessons with him. It is a chance to drop the mom role and get real with him," says Leanne. "Philip takes Kung Fu with Caleb, our other son. It is quite something to be learning something new, being vulnerable alongside your child." Taryn, still a preschooler (and an aspiring ballerina), studies music appreciation with Leanne. Every third Sunday, the family spends the day in the public library. Leanne and Philip have discouraged team sports (although that could change) because "they suck up huge amounts of time."

Most refreshing is Leanne's attitude towards her children's accomplishments. With some prodding, she admitted that Noël is reading at three grade-levels above his class and all the children "do pretty well with their chosen activities." Her lack of effusiveness is a stark contrast to today's tendency of parents to brag *ad nauseam* about their kids. "We refuse to use our kids to compete with other parents," says Leanne. "I find it disturbing how parents go on about their kids."

Competition Is a Fact in the Real World.

"What appears to be competitive parenting is really driven by self-imposed pressure to be the perfect parent—this feeling that you're letting your kids down if you do not provide them with every possible 'perfect' childhood experience: the perfect birthday party, the perfect blend of enriching extracurricular activities: Kindergym, art class, karate, music, swimming lessons, gymnastics, hockey— the list just goes on and on," writes Ann Douglas, author of *The Mother of All Parenting Books* and parent of four children. "This leads to a generation of kids who feel entitled to everything—perhaps because they missed out on the one childhood experience that is most essential of all: the chance to just be a kid. And as for the parents? They are stressed out, burned out, and disillusioned by parenthood. After all, they give everything to their kids and what do they get in return? Kids who want more and appreciate nothing. And for good reason."

Childhood is a time to explore and learn and grow, and a time to fail and win, to dream, develop character and confidence, establish values, and play. It is a time to roam in the world of make-believe, to pause and dream and *just be*. Yes, there is much to learn from team sports, and music lessons instill the important virtue of self-discipline. However, playing in the mud, building castles from sofa cushions and old blankets, and daydreaming under a tree also count as worthwhile things to do.

Kids certainly need all the skills and advantages they can get to make their way in an increasingly complex society, and there is no doubt that achievement and privilege go hand in hand. Gifted children deserve to be encouraged and supported in developing their talents, for they may have much to offer the world. But time with grandma and learning to clean a bathroom matter, too. If a youngster becomes the next great pro-golf champ, she will need practical skills, the ability to relate well to other people, a strong sense of self, and a solid foundation of values to manage life, not just her great swing. Her happiness will depend on it. A healthy life comes down to values, priorities, choices, and balance.

It is sharing time together that cements relationships and sustains love, not dashing off to bassoon lessons, winning gold medals, or achieving Honor Roll standing. While perfecting a triple Lutz might help a child make the national skating team, learning to accept people as they are, respecting others, and developing compassion are fundamental to creating a productive and happy life. And pausing, every day, to be a family matters most.

Although the pressures on kids today are escalating, perhaps the little granddaughter that Steve MacDowall so happily anticipated will be treated, not as a prima donna (unless, of course, she makes it as an opera star), but as a kid who is special and precious, yet a kid just the same. And if she should become the president of a large university, perhaps she will make time to walk with her sweetheart in the morning and pause in the evening for candlelight dinners of macaroni and cheese.

Tips for Family Fun
- Turn off the phones and TV at mealtimes
- Eat at least one meal together daily
- Designate a regular family fun night and get out the Monopoly board
- Pack a lunch and plan a day hike
- Go to the movies together, stop for pizza and chat about what happened on the big screen
- Plan a surprise party to celebrate a special achievement by one of the family
- Cook together
- Pick wild berries and then make jam
- Plan a day to unclutter. Take all your unwanted things to a shelter
- Plant a vegetable garden

- Help at a pet shelter
- Write a family journal that is updated weekly
- Make a monthly trip to the library
- Ride bikes
- Go bowling
- Swim
- Make your Sabbath a family day. Attend church or another faith-based activity. Afterward go for brunch, visit a museum, hike in a park, or bicycle in the country

---

Pause to Ponder
- List your family's priorities (dinners together, celebrating special occasions, attending weekly worship, vacation time?)
- What would you like to do more of? What can you change so this happens?
- How do your work schedule and choice of personal activities affect family time?
- How much time do you spend just hanging out with your special people?
- What do you want your children or grandchildren to remember about their childhoods? How can you create positive memories?
- What family activities give the greatest pleasure?
- How much time do you spend on family fun in a week? In a month?
- How can you schedule more family time?
- How many non-family activities is each member engaged in?
- What do you think the long-term effect would be if one or more of these activities were dropped? Five years from now? Ten years from now?

• We tend to parent in the way we were parented. Are you raising your children in a way you'd like to see your grandchildren raised?

S-L-O-W Food

Good food made with love flavors life.

The darkening sky shudders as Thor rattles the heavens. Rain lashes the windows in clear, cold veins. But inside, the kitchen is warm, filling with the good smells of a simmering stew of carrots, onion, celery, and cubes of seasoned steak. Oh, the delights and convenience of the automatic slow cooker! When we come home we will cut fresh bread in thick slices and share this simple meal. Perfect for a wet and blustery night.

The lunch hour is dead. So is the dinner hour—shrunk to mere minutes or gone altogether. Drinkable soups, instant dinners, cereal bars, pre-washed salads, and pre-sliced apples make eating on the run a crumbless, fussless snap, the perfect accompaniment to our lives in the express lane. Because nearly half of us do not eat at home regularly, quick-fix food suppliers are racing to catch the dine-and-dashers on the fly. Yet pausing to cook, and then enjoy eating every bite, takes the hurry out of the day.

While it might seem the days of simmering stews belong to another era, there is a movement afoot to reinvent the days of pot roast and homemade pie. S-L-O-W is emerging as the latest culinary trend. In 1986, a group of culinary aficionados in the town of Bra, Italy, formed the Slow Food Movement to retaliate against the North American fast-food rage that was infiltrating Europe.

This group of foodies rebelled against the McMeal culture by encouraging its members to grow veggies in the back garden (or buy fresh produce from the farm gate), prepare meals the way grandma did, and make mealtime a celebration of food, friends, and family. Since its inception, interest in slow food has moved beyond Bra. Food lovers around the world are now taking time to cook with hand-picked tomatoes, wild mushrooms, and beans harvested fresh from the vine.

Indulging in the joys of slow cooking gives us delights that go beyond the palate. The Slow Food Movement is the antithesis of the hurried life and goes to the heart of the perfect pause. It puts us in touch with our food as we explore the delights of seasonal ingredients. Cooking for its own sake, not just because we have the munchies, lets us relax into a creative, intimate space where we set aside the bustle of life outside the kitchen to sift and stir. Slow cooking slows down life, putting the concerns outside the kitchen on the back burner. And the smells from the oven are as beneficial as any aromatherapy session.

S-L-O-W Cooking Secrets

If we cannot grow a garden, we can gather the freshest ingredients from a neighborhood market or take a weekend in the country to buy from the good people who tend the land. Ann did just that when she visited a butcher who stocks organic meats. "I had been a vegetarian for so long, so going there was something new to me. I chatted with the owner as he skinned a chicken breast right where I could see him. And then he chopped pork tenderloin into medallions just right for one person. I enjoyed looking around his shop and in his freezer. That little adventure might not seem like much, but for me going there instead of racing into a crowded grocery store, was a lovely leisurely pause."

Fresh ingredients and fun in the kitchen create the magic in slow food. Valerie Sovran Mitchell, author of *Polenta on the Board*, knows the value of both; she was raised on it. Her grandmother, who hailed from Antrodoco, a village in central Italy, brought her traditions with her when she came to North America in the 1920s.

"All hallways led to the kitchen" in her grandmother's home, writes Valerie in the book's introduction. "That is where family life happened. We shared stories, worked out arguments, and I learned the old ways that connected me to a place I had never been. My Nona's kitchen was the center of the home. Always, something wonderful was cooking on the stove."

Perhaps the most endearing recipe in her book is for *polenta*, a dish made from slowly cooked cornmeal, eaten communally in the traditional fashion. "One of the main pieces of equipment in grandmother's kitchen was a huge board which Papa made in his basement workshop," she writes. "Nona kept it meticulously cleaned and carefully oiled and, over time, the board deepened to a rich golden color. It always carried the scent of fresh-baked bread." She tells of how the board was set in the center of the table. Thick, steaming polenta was spread over it, topped with "long-simmering tomato sauce with sausages or spareribs or meatballs, and cheese." The family would pull up their chairs, grab their forks, and dig in.

Valerie's deep appreciation of her heritage flavors her

food and her life. Although she is every bit a modern woman, she considers the nurturing qualities of food preparation integral to her well-being. "Whatever I am cooking—it might be soup or something like *vitello indoratto* (veal with lemon and eggs)—I put on music that matches my mood, sometimes opera, sometimes reggae. I dance and sing as I cook. The crushing, pounding, kneading, stirring, choosing complementary ingredients, taste, texture and color, all this makes cooking so creative. Whether I cook for others or just for myself, it is an expressive act. Quite simply, cooking makes me happy.

"People who understand my passion for cooking often ask why I'm not seriously overweight," says Valerie. "I tell them that preparing food is something apart from eating. But I like that, too! When food is served I savor each bite, take pleasure in the taste, and really experience the food. We don't have to eat huge portions to do that."

Uncle Julio's Lentil Soup

Uncle Julio saves the rind for parmigiano cheese to add to hearty soups and sauces as they simmer. It enhances the flavor in a subtle but distinctively rustic way.

2 tbsp (30 ml) finely chopped yellow onion
4 tbsp (60 ml) extra virgin olive oil
3 tbsp (45 ml) butter
2 tbsp (30 ml) each finely chopped celery and
    carrots
1/8 lb (60 g) prosciutto, diced or shredded
1 cup (250 ml) canned plum tomatoes, roughly
    chopped
1/2 lb (250 g) brown lentils, rinsed and drained
5 cups (1.2 L) beef broth

2 cups (500 ml) water
salt and freshly ground pepper
rind of parmigiano cheese (if available)
4 tbsp (60 ml) grated parmigiano cheese

In a large pot, sauté onions in the oil and butter at medium heat for 8-10 minutes, or until they are soft and lightly golden.

Add celery and carrots and simmer for 3-4 minutes, stirring regularly to prevent burning. Add the prosciutto and sauté for another minute.

Add chopped tomatoes and their juice and simmer for 30 minutes, stirring from time to time. Add the rinsed and drained lentils and stir.

Stir in 4 cups (1.2 L) of broth (reserving one cup) and the water. Add 6 or 7 grindings of pepper, salt to taste (the prosciutto adds saltiness so be careful not to over-salt), and add the parmigiano rind.

Simmer slowly for 50 to 60 minutes, checking after 40 minutes and adding more broth if the soup is too thick. Remove the parmigiano rind before serving. Pass the grated cheese

(courtesy of Valerie Sovran Mitchell)

David, a chef in a small Montreal establishment, echoed Valerie's passionate approach to cooking. "There needs to be love for the food," he said as he wrapped salmon steaks in filo pastry. "Of course, it's also about understanding how ingredients work together, but it's most important to care about what you're cooking and those who will eat it. You can't bottle that, and you will not find it in a recipe book. But you'll know when it is missing."

Cooking and eating with others is good therapy. It brings people together. It is a time to pause and drop the roles we play in the outside world and just hang out. Sadly, research shows that families who eat together regularly are the exception. In our runaway world of packed schedules, weeks, even months, can pass without a family eating together. Many newly designed homes have done away with space for the kitchen table in favor of a sit-up counter, perfect for the quick snack, but hardly the setting to encourage conversation.

Second Helpings

Miriam Weinstein, author of *The Surprising Power of Family Meals: How Eating Together Makes Us Smarter, Stronger, Healthier, and Happier*, speaks of how we are missing out on life's little lessons by not pausing to eat together. "Sharing family meals teaches children the art of conversation, etiquette, and table manners, skills that become increasingly important as they reach maturity and go out into the world," she says. "Knowing which fork to use and how to negotiate a business lunch can determine whether we are suitable for a promotion or not. Some corporations now take prospective employees to dinner to assess their social skills."

Her book underlines how we have become so focused on commitments outside the home that we forfeit time together, the very essence of what makes a family. "I know it's difficult, but we need to carve time from our busy schedules to talk with each other and to physically be with each other," says Miriam. "A family that travels together over time has a sense of connection."

She describes how parents in Wayzata, Minnesota, fought to take back family time: "Sitting down and eating a meal one night a week with all members present was a huge challenge," says Barbara Carlson, a Wayzata resident who with others formed the organization Putting Family First. "We learned that only 31 percent of families eat meals together on a regular basis and 58 percent of those have the TV on!" The movement is gaining attention far beyond their community.[12]

With the invasion of televisions in almost every room (including the kitchen) and the ease of grabbing a pre-packaged dinner from the freezer, we have migrated from the kitchen to the couch. "If you can do only one thing with those you care about, eat a meal with them," Barbara urges. She believes a table that is filled with good things to eat and surrounded by happy people is the best place on Earth: it is where we tell stories, pass on traditions, and simply enjoy being together.

Wayzata parents have successfully encouraged school administrators and those in charge of after-school activities to acknowledge the importance of family commitments. The football coach supports them by ensuring football practice ends in time for dinner. (Other schools they compete against have teams that often practice until 7:30 p.m.) "At the beginning of the season, he calls the parents and players together to emphasize his coaching priorities," said Barbara. "He says it straight: faith, family, schoolwork, then football. He's a tough coach and a winning coach and he expects the kids to give their all, but he puts things like family vacations, weddings, and funerals before practices and games."

Just as food and family are natural companions, so are food and friends. Carolyn, a busy literary agent, tempers the pressures of negotiating author contracts and fielding endless phone calls by taking occasional weekends to cook with a friend. "I have such pleasant times with Heather, catching up on our lives over the soup pot. We love to get together and cook, laugh, drink wine, and eat," she says with a smile in her voice. "There's no competition to make things perfect. The purpose is just being together." She adds that, because her friend chooses not to have a dishwasher, they have the pleasure of looking over the landscape while washing up. "Herons swoop down and ferries go by. The entire experience is absolutely wonderful."

Even though we might not have a fish market at the end of our street or a garden in which to grow tomatoes, we can turn off the TV, unplug the phone, open a cookbook, and disappear into our own world of S-L-O-W. When we pause to peel potatoes, slice carrots, and create our own version of slow food, we make cooking a joy, not a duty, and put goodness in our tummies and love in our lives, every day.

Dining-in Guidelines

- Strive to eat one meal a day together as a family
- Eat at a table. Light candles and toast the day
- Make mealtime fun. Leave heavy topics for later
- No distractions: turn off the phones, television, and radio
- Everyone lends a hand either with cooking or cleaning up. Rotate the tasks
- Be a slow food slough-off. If the day looks busy, put a stew in the Crock Pot (also marketed as a slow cooker) early in the morning. At dinnertime, toss together a salad, slice up some fresh bread, dish out the stew, and you are ready to eat

Pause to Ponder
- Where in your community can you buy fresh ingredients grown locally?
- Does someone in your neighborhood offering cooking classes for ethnic dishes, soup- or bread-making?
- Commit time and care to preparing, serving, and eating to make the evening meal a special pause in the day. What rituals can you incorporate into this time?
- If you live alone, try to make at least one meal a week a time to connect with family or friends.
- Learn to make soup from scratch; it's easy, wholesome, and cheap!
- Consider the many hands that brought your meal to the table. Give thanks for the farmers, harvesters, truckers, and others who helped make the meal possible.

Brain-buffing

Use it or lose it.

We are sitting in a classroom on the second floor of the neighborhood high school. The place triggers memories of long-ago afternoons when a well-meaning teacher tried but failed to teach me French. Back then, rules for sentence structure, grammatical nuances, and verbs flew over my head while I plotted ways to conjugate my way out of her class—which eventually I did.

But now I am back at school sitting with a pack of others ready (and willing!) to delve into the mysteries of la langue français.

I am motivated by the many puzzled faces that stared back at me when I first visited France: I had fumbled my way through menus I could not read and further embarrassed myself (and amused the hotel clerk) when I asked for a "single room with two toilets" when I meant "a double room with a shower."

In classrooms down the hall from ours, others are learning about photography, creative writing, Greek drama, and Turkish archaeological digs. These evenings are brief interludes from our regular lives, pauses where we buff our brains and have fun doing it.

Joan was new in the city when we met at a travel-writing course. "At my age, you have to keep your brain well-oiled," she said. "The old saying, use it or lose it, is no joke." Joan, who was celebrating her eighty-ninth birthday that year, traveled widely and had lived in a number of countries. She wanted to write about her adventures and meet others who, like her, wanted to learn the fine points of putting stories together. What fun she was, injecting our sessions with witty tales of airport miscues and cultural mishaps in Africa, Australia, and the Far East. By the end of the six-week course, she had met her goals: she had new friends and a solid understanding of what it takes to interest a publisher.

Joan's curiosity about the world and her courage to put herself among people decades younger were a great inspiration. "A body's gotta take time to learn something new every day, meet people, and get out of the house," she told us. "Even if it is just ten minutes to check on the specials down at the food mart."

Joan's advice must have merit. She was as sharp as anyone in the class and nearly as energetic. Pausing to buff our brains might seem a waste of time in our overly committed lives, but a few minutes a day is good fun, and a very smart thing to do.

Brain-buffing 101

Jog your mind. When we pause to learn new things, we enliven our days and increase our brain power. The comfort of familiar situations is seductive as we humans prefer routines and feel most confident and at ease with faces, places, and activities we know. But that's no way to brain-buff. Neurologists argue (and Joan proves) that we can remain as sharp as a tack well into old age if we exercise our gray matter. This means turning off the TV to play card games, doing crossword puzzles, studying Spanish, or learning to play bridge. Whenever we ask questions (and then seek out answers), we flex our brains. If we pause to question what the mystics mean when they challenge us to make tea from an empty cup, or learn the difference between a sonata and a concerto, or investigate whether or not geese mourn the loss of their own, we get a mental workout.

Research by Marion C. Diamond indicates that continuous challenges to the brain build stronger, more agile mental functions. Her findings show that we have "a pigment called lipofuscin that accumulates in our brains as we age. It is thought to interfere with the normal function of the nerve cells." She argues we can beat back our production of lipofuscin if we regularly try new activities and take on new challenges.[13] It is encouraging to note that people who frequently do mentally stimulating activities have a reduced risk of Alzheimer's disease.[14]

Most age-related loss of memory or motor skills results from inactivity and a lack of mental exercise. Challenging the brain through new activities creates stronger dendrites, branch-like conduits that are integral to our ability to learn and remember. Dendrites grow and thicken with new experiences, and the thicker the better!

Round up the free radicals. In 1954, Dr. Denham Harman, co-founder of the International Association of Biomedical Gerontology, discovered some nasty little devils he called free radicals. These are produced in the body when a cell, which is held together by electrical bonds, becomes unstable. Free radicals damage healthy cells and cause signs of premature aging such as wrinkles and joint stiffness. They also contribute to more than fifty known ailments including cancer, heart disease, cataracts, and Alzheimer's—a primary cause of admission to nursing homes. The list keeps growing.

Chronic stress, insufficient sleep (which also impairs the immune system), fast-food, exposure to excessive sunlight, environmental pollution, lack of essential nutrients in the diet, and smoking are major contributors to free-radical growth. A single puff of a cigarette floods the brain with thousands of harmful chemicals that feed free-radical formation. If we value our brains, we'll butt out. And we will also pass on recreational drugs and resist drinking more than two alcoholic drinks a day.

But even if we've been a chain-smoking, beer-swilling, chips-and-hotdog kind of person for decades, if we pause and adopt a healthier diet and fine-tune our lifestyle, we can repair and pump up our brain power while improving our overall health.

Binge on brain food. Pause to eat smart. "Food is a powerful medicine," writes neurologist David Perlmutter in *The Better Brain Book.* He insists we load up on "brain-building" foods that are rich in antioxidants (the good guys that combat the effects of free radicals). At the top of the list are foods containing vitamin E, beta carotene (converted in the body to vitamin A), and vitamin C. These are found in many fruits and vegetables.

Researchers with the U.S. Department of Agriculture suggest that dried beans, wild blueberries, strawberries, cooked artichokes, prunes, apples, and Russet potatoes are among a number of fruits and vegetables that offer significant amounts of antioxidants. However, just how much antioxidant clout our body absorbs has not been fully determined. [15]

Omega 3-enriched eggs, spinach, seeds, and nuts (especially walnuts and walnut oil) are also potent in fighting free radicals. The trace metal selenium increases the effectiveness of our antioxidant enzyme system, but can be difficult to obtain naturally. A supplement of 30 milligrams a day is recommended. Also co-enzyme Q10, a powerful antioxidant produced in the body—but which decreases as we age, is enormously important to the brain and can also be taken as a supplement. (Please consult your doctor first.)

Sleep and get smart. Think of time in bed as beauty sleep for the brain. Adequate sleep (between eight and nine hours in a 24-hour period) is essential for good brain health. Over time, cheating on sleep will shortchange our brain cells. Dr. Perlmutter writes, "Losing even one night's sleep has a marked physiological effect on the body," and that "missing sleep doesn't just make us feel lousy, it can cause long-term damage to your brain cells." When the body is at rest, the brain rejuvenates and cleans out the sludge caused by free radicals. This is also when the body tunes up the immune system.

Get hip and knit. Pause to de-stress. Teenagers, working women and men (yes, even such he-men as Russell Crowe) are discovering why knitting is kind to the mind. The rhythmic motion and pace of knitting makes it balm for our over-stressed culture, a Tai Chi for the mind. That is a good thing. Stress is a silent brain bomb. Daniel Amen, a professor of psychiatry and human behavior at the University of California, argues that, "Stress hormones kill brain cells in the memory and cause serious trouble for other organs in the body. Just realizing that and deciding to work on reducing stress is a good step." Managing our stress levels means taking control of our lives minute by minute. If knitting isn't our thing, library shelves are stacked with books that focus on stress reduction. Here are five points to consider:

• *Write it down*. Writing often clarifies a situation and promotes a solution. Putting troubling issues down on
paper transfers them from our heads to where we can
look at them more clearly.

• *Take action*. Deciding to resolve a problem, rather than
stewing about it, reduces its power over us and eases
the stress it generates. Seek out a wise and trusted
friend, or consult a professional to help you.

• *Forget multi-tasking*. Tackle one thing at a time and set
aside enough time to complete the task. Doing too
much or too many tasks at once generates confusion
and anxiety.

• *Consider a stress-reducing hobby*. Try an activity that is
opposite to what you usually do. If you are the cerebral
type, try something physical. If you have jock tenden-
cies, pick up a book. Other hobbies might include
painting, gardening, writing your memoir, delving into
your family history, sewing, woodworking, building
model ships, or pottery.

Pause every day. Regular breaks to hit a tennis ball, read
something funny, create an original recipe, or just sit on a
bench all give our heads and hearts a mini-vacation. *Work
it out*. Pause to perspire. Research shows that working out
three times a week provides significant protection against
Alzheimer's and reduces stress. While vigorous exercise is
most beneficial, even low-intensity exercise is a brain-
booster. Any exercise—walking, swimming, bicycling, gardening, Tai Chi, yoga—that gets the body moving and the
heart pumping increases blood flow and nutrition to the
brain. Physical activity also boosts our creativity. Solutions
to problems often pop into our heads when we get up and
move. Ernest Hemingway is said to have walked the streets

of Paris when contemplating the perfect word.

Making time to buff our brains puts juice into the day. When my elderly friend Joan learned to write about travel, she also made new friends, had a story published in a small local magazine, and wrote her autobiography. Rather than wind down her life, she is revving it up. I have not seen her recently, but wherever she is, she is likely to be asking questions, taking on new challenges, and enjoying an occasional pause somewhere exotic.

Daily Tips to Buff Your Brain
- Select a foreign language and learn five words each day
- Memorize a quote a day by someone you admire (libraries and bookstores sell books of quotations and there are plenty on the Internet)
- Television is brain candy. Get out the puzzles or learn to play chess
- Play cards or Scrabble
- Try Tai Chi as exercise for the body and brain
- Eat a prune a day
- Take a hike
- Walk backwards
- Sleep tight, every night
- Do less and reduce stress
- Change your travel routes and routines

Pause to Ponder
- What fun activity would you like to learn? Go for it!
- Routines can be brain-numbing. Do you go to the same vacation spot each year? Consider a change and feel your dendrites grow with the new challenges.
- Why not find new routes to work, sit in a different pew on Sunday, try an unfamiliar recipe, eat in a new restaurant, or brush your teeth with the opposite hand?

Between the Sheets

"No day is so bad it can't be fixed with a nap."
Comic Carrie Snow has it right on!

The most delicious part of the day comes in the late afternoon when I turn off the computer and unplug the phone. That is when I make a cup of tea and curl up on the sofa for a thirty-minute period of self-indulgent rest. I might read a bit, snooze, or just let my mind wander. It is a quiet transition into the next phase of the day, a private, very precious pause.

I am not the only one admitting to late-afternoon idleness. Judy, a freelance writer, naps with her cats. "Every afternoon, I plop on the bed under a comforter, two cats snuggling at my feet, and drift away in refreshing slumber. I only sleep about a half-hour or so, but I feel much better when I wake up."

Artist Robert Bateman, who captures the wonders of the natural world on canvases that hang in some of the world's most renowned galleries, also rests every day. "I can sleep in the busiest places, even on the floor of O'Hare Airport," he says. Now that's an accomplishment! When he is not traveling, he sleeps in his bed from twenty to forty minutes most afternoons. Although well into his 70s, he looks and acts years younger, keeps a full schedule of painting and speaking, and makes significant contributions of his time to environmental organizations. While the demands on him are fierce, so is his commitment to his daily snooze. "I began napping when I was a young teacher in Africa. Siestas were the norm there and I have kept the habit since then," he tells me.

Not all of us have cats to warm our toes, nor do we all control our own schedules. Working in an office means conforming to a corporate or institutional regimen where putting up our feet and closing our eyes for a midday pause could mean a boot out the door. But attitudes in the workplace, even among large corporations, are changing as they recognize the link between employee wellness and productivity. Sleep is more significant than we may realize.

Asleep on the Job

Writer Marianne Scott, who specializes in the marine industry, was stunned to see an entire boat-building plant come to a full stop on the day she visited it. "I was touring a factory in Taiwan when the lunch bell sounded. I was astounded to see 150 men eat their lunches and then, wherever they happened to be, lie down and sleep for the remainder of the hour."

She describes that visit in the book *Ocean Alexander: The First 25 Years*. "Ocean Alexander's crew works more hours than either their North American or European counterparts. They are on the job by 7:30 a.m., leave at 5:30 p.m., and work every other Saturday. A blast of music announces coffee breaks and lunchtime. At noon, everyone downs tools and turns off the machines. Most people relax and eat the food they bring to work, but they do not spend the entire lunch hour eating. After putting away their lunch pails, they stretch out on or under tables, on top of stacks of wood—wherever there is a convenient spot—and snooze, their dust masks now doing duty as eyeshades. Even the office staff naps, their heads resting on the desk next to the keyboard. At 1:00 p.m., another musical explosion warns it is time to resume work. Everyone flips the 'on' button on their machine and returns to their tasks, refreshed.

"Studies show midday naps increase worker productivity, improve problem-solving, and lower accident rates. Perhaps the Ocean Alexander team can teach North Americans and Europeans a thing or two [about the importance of rest]."

But could such a habit exist in North American industry? Gary, a stockbroker with a large Canadian financial institution, proves it can: "At 2:00 p.m., I close the office door and zone out for fifteen or twenty minutes. I have been napping every day for years. My boss and the guys I work with know I do this, and yeah, they might snicker, but I carry on." Gary exhibits a perfectly normal need. Studies confirm our bodies yearn for rest in the afternoon and that we fall asleep most easily between 2:00 p.m. and 3:00 p.m. As for Gary's job performance? He is one of the top producers in the business.

While Gary and the well-rested Taiwanese take their daily naps, studies show that more than half of North Americans—65 percent—are fighting sleep deprivation. In today's clock-driven culture, we sleep an average of 7.5 hours, two hours less than we did prior to 1913, when electricity became widely accessible, and 1.5 hours less than primates in the wild. Our techno-playthings entice us to spend an average of 1.18 hours daily on the Internet, with more than half of that time taken from between the sheets. Combine this with the lure of video games, a daily average of four hours of watching television, and longer hours at work, and it is no wonder we wander around tired and cranky.

Insufficient sleep might make us less fun to be with, but it also compromises our productivity, slows our reaction times, and makes us less focused. This puts us at risk of accidents when we drive and is behind many workplace accidents. Whatever we might think, most of us need nine hours of sleep within each twenty-four-hour period.

In the introduction to his book *Sleep Thieves*, Dr. Stanley Coren writes, "What do the nuclear accident at Chernobyl, the near meltdown at Three Mile Island, and the disastrous oil spill of the *Exxon Valdez* have in common? They were all caused by people who were making mistakes because they had had too little sleep."[16]

More recently, an investigation into the crash of a small plane into Lake Erie that killed ten people blamed pilot stress for a series of errors. According to a May 2006 article in *Aviation Now*, an investigation by Canada's Transportation Safety Board reported that the pilot's assessment of risk was likely degraded by some combination of stress and fatigue. The pilot had slept only five hours the night before the fatal crash.

One in five drivers admits to having nodded off at the wheel at least once in the past year, according to a new survey conducted by the Ottawa-based Traffic Injury Research Foundation.
Source: U.S. National Sleep Foundation

Dr. Coren's research so convinced him that sleep was a

necessity, an essential pause, that he bumped up his own down time. "Eight hours at night is the absolute minimum for me," he says, "and I usually take a short afternoon nap as well." He cites a study that followed a group of environmental researchers to the High Arctic during midsummer when the sun doesn't set. The group had the scientific equipment they needed but no time-keeping devices. They were encouraged to ignore a sleep schedule and to rest whenever they felt the need. Interestingly, they slept an average of 10.3 hours, about the same as primates in the wild.

The U.S. National Commission on Sleep Disorders estimates that the direct cost of sleep disorders and sleep deprivation is $15.9 billion dollars. It estimates $50 billion to $100 billion in direct and indirect costs related to accidents caused by lack of sleep.

Our round-the-clock culture fights sleep as if it were an enemy. We have enshrined the idea that tough guys do not sleep and that sack time is for wimps. The attitude of bravado surrounding lack of sleep is said to have begun with the American inventor Thomas Edison, the man responsible for commercial development of the sleep-curtailing light bulb. Edison boasted he slept just four hours a night, but, according to Dr. Coren, he took two naps during the day.

Much has been made of Winston Churchill's legendary stamina, based on claims he also slept just four or five hours a night. As with Edison, there is more to the story. He may not have slept much at night but during World War II, Churchill apparently kept an army cot in his bunker that he used every afternoon—after changing into his pajamas!

Perhaps these daily naps were a factor in Edison's and Churchill's brilliance. A University of Amsterdam study suggests that complex decisions are best made when we gather all the information we can and then forget about the problem. The study claims that if we pause, and let our subconscious minds work out a solution we are likely to arrive at more creative options. Perhaps Edison and Churchill were hard at work even when they were snug between the sheets?

Our Elusive Dreams

For many of us, a runaway life means a good night's sleep is an elusive dream.

Today's status symbols include not only the size of our homes or the make of our cars, but also how busy we are—and how tired we feel. We are simply doing too much, too fast. We feel lazy if we are not rushing out the door, swamped in work, or juggling conflicting commitments. Our inner and outer lives are whirling at such a rate that we cannot power down. But there are other factors that contribute to sleeplessness.

Our fondness for extra-tall coffees and late-night alcohol, over-working and the lure of the television conspire to steal precious sleep time. A mere half-hour less a night creates a significant shortage by the week's end. If we play hard on Saturday and Sunday, we start the following week with a deficit. If that continues, we begin to break down by degrees until our bodies protest in ways we cannot ignore.

Fatigue Facts

Ongoing studies in endocrinology point to a relationship between sleep and metabolism. It appears that the less we sleep the fatter we get.

Although the connection between sleep and weight gain is complex, certain studies indicate that hormones which control feelings of hunger are miscued when we are sleep-deprived, tempting us to eat more often than we ordinarily would.[17]

Sleep deprivation has consequences that go beyond a yawn or two:

- We become less productive
- Our abilities to solve problems and to concentrate are reduced
- We become more accident-prone
- We become forgetful, less alert, and cranky
- We are less able to handle daily stress
- We have less restorative time for body and mind
- Our immune system is compromised
- We get more colds, flu, and infections

Sleepless in the Nursery

Of startling concern is sleeplessness in children. Nearly 70 percent of youngsters are experiencing problems in this area, ranging from trouble settling down to bed-wetting.[18] In her excellent book *Sleep Solutions for Your Baby, Toddler, and Preschooler: The Ultimate No-Worry Approach for Each Age and Stage,* Ann Douglas writes that our schedules (and our children's) are becoming so frantic our kids cannot decompress. Like their parents, kids do best when they sleep in their own bed with a regular schedule for naps and bedtime. "Of course, there are times we can't hold to a schedule," says Ann. "We might need to dash out for groceries when it is nap time, but one thing is for sure, when kids skip their naps or have irregular schedules, they soon become sleep-deprived with all the attendant problems."

She says that children can become whiny, clinging, irritable, uncooperative, and aggressive with siblings and playmates. Makes me think of some overtired adults I know!

Ann also cautions us to read our children carefully and take action before they become overtired. She also believes that sleep deprivation is a possible cause of Attention Deficit Disorder and disruptive behavior in school-aged children. "Kids are simply exhausted. They, like their parents, need a pause during the day, a quiet time for rest or sleep, and a schedule that respects their physical and mental limits." Sadly, for some children it isn't enough to say that if they get enough sleep they will behave in the classroom, but kids without underlying mental health problems will benefit from a proper sleep schedule.

While some sleep issues are physical or psychological in origin, two significant contributors are easy to avoid: caffeinated beverages, and televisions in the bedroom. (More than 40 percent of school-aged children have a television in their bedroom.) According to the U.S. National Sleep Foundation, "about 26 percent of children between the ages of three and ten drink at least one caffeinated beverage a day [this includes some soft drinks and chocolate]; plus they sleep less than those who do not drink caffeine (9.1 versus 9.7 hours a night), for a loss of about 3.5 hours a week."

Sleep is a non-negotiable pause, an essential element in putting the brakes on a runaway life. Getting sufficient time between the sheets is the basis for physical health and an essential ingredient for mental acuity. And it is a wonder remedy. An old Irish proverb puts it succinctly: "A good laugh and a long sleep are the best cures in the doctor's book." So, off to bed!

Tips to Sleep Better

- Develop regular sleep habits throughout the week, including weekends
- Establish a relaxing bedtime routine such as bathing, reading, or listening to music
- Create a sleep-conducive environment that is dark, quiet, comfortable, and cool
- Sleep on a comfortable mattress
- Keep the bedroom just for sleeping and cuddling. Remove the television and computer
- Finish eating at least two to three hours before bed
- Exercise regularly. It is best to complete your workout a couple of hours before bedtime
- No alcohol, caffeine, and nicotine near bedtime
- Take a daily nap, if only for fifteen minutes
- Contact the National Sleep Foundation at (202) 347-3471, or visit *www.sleepfoundation.org*

Source: U.S. National Sleep Foundation

Pause to Ponder

- What is your attitude towards taking a nap?
- Who or what influences these?
- How much sleep time do you average in a twenty-four-hour period?
- How might you arrange your routine to make more time for rest?

Playful Pauses ...

can be delightful, decadent, curious, or edgy

Getting silly is a good thing, and so is munching on caramel-covered popcorn and stealing away to see an afternoon movie. Lingering over brunch on a Sunday morning, playing tourist in the town where we live, and occasionally spoiling ourselves rotten puts zing into life. Playful pauses keep us happy and in tune with the kid inside. They remind us that incidental and sometimes seemingly insignificant moments give life its vibrancy and its zest.

We may not be able to change how we live or what we do to pay the rent, but we can top up the day with a little decadence, a little self-indulgence. So grab a special coffee on the way to work, pop out for lunch with someone who makes you laugh, and take a detour along a lovely street on the way home. Joyful pauses are the chocolate sprinkles of life and we deserve heaps of them—every day.

That Sweet Pause

Love does more than put stars in our eyes;
it makes life a grand, unforgettable adventure.

Bud the Tile Guy bounces into my house. He's a big man, all brawny and bulging and good-looking. His dark hair is short, highlighted with blond streaks. Two iron-ring earrings and a wee bit of chin fluff distinguish this man who is here to improve the look of the bathroom. Bud, who is single and closing in on middle age, is in a talkative mood and before long his life history is on the table (while the floor tiles wait nearby). In a torrent of breathless sentences, he described a life jammed with commitments. "I need to have a bunch of projects on the go. I live to work. If I'm not busy, I look for something to do. I think nothing of working from early morning to midnight."

After hours he dashes off to play golf or meet the guys at the hockey rink. As for his love life, he says he is keen to meet the right woman but, "I guess I'm not very good marriage material." He says this to explain his single status. "The ex-wife said I was just too busy, had too many things going on. That's my story: too busy, too many things. I guess you gotta be around more to make a marriage work!"

That encounter with Bud reminded me that making time for our special people is the secret to sustaining our heart-life, for these are the folks who hang out with us *just because*.

An editor pal of mine confirmed this when he told me how working in a large city many miles from home was bearable for him because of a friend he made who shared his passion for sports. The guys had fun going to pro games or watching them on the tube. Before long they were wondering whether to join a dragon-boat crew for a summer-fun event. My friend was describing what I refer to as life's "sweet pauses," but he also commented that these happy times did not just happen. The two buddies work at creating gaps in their packed schedules so they can kick back and relax. That "work" is the feeding and watering needed to make all relationships thrive, for it takes more than e-mailing seasonal best wishes as each year-end rolls around to sustain meaningful friendships.

Looking at current divorce statistics, boosted as they are by the tragedy of alcohol and drug addictions, it becomes clear that society has moved away from the traditional families portrayed in such once-popular TV shows as *Leave It to Beaver* and *Father Knows Best*. With more and more of us poised to spend at least some part of our adulthood without a main squeeze, the support system of good friendships becomes an essential element in our emotional well-being. Just ask any struggling single parent!

As we chatted about friendship, my pal mused that, for him, having a "sports buddy" is not the same as having a partner-in-life. This punster divorcé, who cherishes the institution of marriage, agreed to make the split with his first bride final after a prolonged period of separation. He readily admitted that he was looking forward to having another "altar ego."

What's Love Got to Do with It?

Like a slow waltz, a sweet pause tingles the senses. It is filled with surprises and coated in courtesy. Like a growing garden, our special relationships thrive on sweet pauses. Despite our best intentions, our dearest people can sometimes be left in the wake of our hurried lives as we end our day tired and in no mood for going to a ball game or playing footsie under the table. On average, many of us spend less than an hour a week in meaningful conversation with our partners. As Bud learned, that is not a recipe for a successful relationship. We will have better odds of keeping our lovers at our side if we commit to even thirty minutes of uninterrupted chat time daily, a couple of hour-long, heart-to-heart conversations each week, and an overnight getaway every two or three months. Occasional longer rendezvous each year (leave the kids) will give a twosome enough sweet pauses to help keep love alight.

Harriet and Robert have been together for twenty-six years and still anticipate their weekly dates. "When we were both working, we'd end our week on Fridays at noon. Our routine was pretty regular: we met at the same place for lunch (with absolutely yummy pecan pie), and, this was our one rule, we never talked about the kids," says Harriet with a grin. "This was time for us."

Now when they go out, they put on their "date clothes" and make whatever they do an event. "For us, putting on something nice gives us a sense of occasion—makes it seem special—even if we're just going to a movie."

Harriet explains the strength of their relationship rests on how they treat each other: "Throughout our marriage we've had highs and downs, but we are very kind to each other, and generous with our money and our time. We wait on each other and try to share the chores. Neither of us is carrying the load alone."

Murray and Duane, who are parenting two sons, commit to season tickets to the opera. "Because these evenings are already booked, they are 'fixed.' It's so easy for other things to creep into our schedules, and the boys keep us pretty busy. This way, we get at least some time away from our regular responsibilities."

Another couple I know took up ballroom dancing as a surefire way to build in relationship time. Once a week, they slip into their dancing shoes, wrap their arms around each other, and float across the floor. "We're busy with our jobs during the week," one says, "and dancing puts us together. It's really fun, even though I was a real klutz at first. And we've met some great people."

Tender Loving Care

Even though special relationships are precious, they can be easy to overlook, brush aside, or take for granted. This is something Steve and Beverly are unlikely to do.

"Do you remember the first time you met your love-to-be? I do," writes Steve MacDowall in his weekly e-newsletter, *The Thursday File*. [10]

"More than thirty years ago, friends who wanted me to join them on a trip to Wisconsin interrupted me while I was working on a watercolor portrait of a mare and her colt. I was reluctant, but they finally cajoled me into making the journey.

"It changed my life.

"They took me to a house on Taco Street in Neenah-Menasha. It was early in the morning and we went around the back and up what seemed to be dozens of steps. It was in that house that I first met Beverly. As corny as it sounds, the next day I actually wrote in a diary, 'I'm going to marry her.'

"Miss Beverly, however, was not as receptive. Despite my efforts to persuade her what a nice fellow I was, I got the cold shoulder. My friends rallied around and assured me 'she likes you.' When I arrived home I finished my painting and dated it the day I first saw Beverly. I presented it to her on my second visit the following month. We got married in Toronto a little over six months after our first encounter.

"I do not think I will ever forget the first time I saw my love-to-be, but if my memory gets a bit fuzzy, I just have to look at the painting."

When I think of Steve and Beverly, I sense his affection for her as something very precious, very sweet. It is as if they are engaged in a dance for two—a steamy tango, a playful polka, a raucous rock and roll, whatever they want it to be. But always, I bet, it is fun, frolicsome and unforgettable, a fairytale dusted with enchanting encounters.

I enjoy watching couples that have had many happy years together, or friends who have a shared history. They seem to move to a rhythm only they can hear. Other signs tell me all is well: a smile that speaks a private language, a perfect apple cut and cored and served as a surprise, a newspaper carefully positioned with breakfast; a cup of tea served just the way she likes it. Little courtesies, little pauses of thoughtfulness, keep things sweet. So does good old-fashioned laughter: nothing keeps a relationship more vibrant than a healthy hoot.

Along with treating our special person with gentle courtesy and unfailing respect, laughter is a potent source of relationship sustenance. It strengthens our sense of togetherness as we share a moment that is uniquely ours. Laughter keeps our bodies healthy, too. In his book *Anatomy of an Illness*, Norman Cousins, who used laughter to help him conquer a life-threatening illness, calls it "internal jogging." When we laugh, we instantly bond with those who chuckle with us. Tense or trying situations are defused. As our heart rate momentarily increases and then relaxes, so does our blood pressure. Out pour the "feel-good" hormones that can reduce pain and boost our immune system. Not only is a good laugh tonic for a relationship, it massages facial muscles and gives our diaphragm and abdomen a workout.

Yucking it up has no downside (unless we use humor to belittle others). So take your sweetheart's hand and go for a walk. But don't just hold hands, swing them high and then higher until you feel like you did when you were a kid. And then laugh all the way down the street.

From twirls on the dance floor to games on the soccer field, creative play heightens the tempo of our personal lives and keeps things interesting. Without a shot of fun, our time together can become boring and missing the invigorating escapades that entice us back for more.

A happy love life flavors life. It helps us handle the pressures of unpredictable events. When we pause to express affection, and know we are accepted and treasured by people we respect and value, we can handle disappointments more easily and will feel better about the world and about ourselves. It is the pause that keeps life sweet and it is worth all the twirling and dipping we can muster.

Sweet Pauses

The surprise. Adding a few juniper berries to a stew gives it an edgy twist. Including the unexpected in a relationship also pumps it up. Stop by the deli for picnic goodies and spring an unexpected lunch on your special person. You might steal away to a park or skip off to the seashore in the middle of the week. Show up with tickets for a great con-cert, arrange a weekend away to a secret location, or announce "it's pajama day" and stay home (and in bed) with your sweetie. Wherever you do, make it informal, spontaneous, and simple.

Walk talk. Taking a walk together at the end of the day gives a relationship focused attention. Not only will we walk off the day's stress, we also create an opportunity for that all-important verbal foreplay that could lead towards togeth-erness of the more physically intimate kind.

Playtime. Recreate your childhood by spending an afternoon at the water park, playing pick-up sticks after dinner, tossing a Frisbee in the park.

On Saturdays, Rosie and James play in the park near her home. With GPS in hand, they are among thousands roaming through cities, parks, the countryside, and around buildings looking for "geocaches" (the phrase is taken from "geography" and "caching") placed there by others in this latest date game.[19] More than 300,000 active caches are up for grabs in countries around the world. Cache-seekers are poking into unsuspected corners for entertaining "treas-ures" hidden by other geocaching junkies.

"Geocaching gives us a reason to get out and walk," says Rosie. "James is the outdoor type and knows so much about trees and stuff. I've learned a lot about him. We talk more, solve problems together, and really have a blast. We've got a quest, a mission. And because there are loads of geocaches in the area where we live, we can do it any-time." She says that although a GPS system is good to have, a compass works just as well. "And you really learn the names of the trees," giggles Rosie.

If geocaching is not your thing, what outdoor adventure would summon your Tarzan or Jane?

Go tube-less. My husband and I have business commitments that take us away from each other frequently. When we are home, we eliminate distractions that get in the way of our time together. One of these is the TV. We are part of the growing group that has unplugged the tube. (We love movies and so keep a VCR and DVD.) Not everyone wants to throw out the tube, but a vacation from the TV a few nights a week opens time up for walks and talks and much, much more. On average, North Americans spend 23 hours a week watching TV. That's a lot of time that might be filled with some very sweet pauses!

Hammers and nails. Working together on projects opens up the laugh lines. Clean out the garage, plan and then plant a garden, paint the fence, or build a porch. Sand an old table, refinish it, and then toast your work.

Nighty-night. A good-morning kiss and nighttime cuddle start and end the day on a lovely note. Yet we may find we are too rushed or too tired to offer even this. By resisting the temptation to work late or watch TV and hitting the sack instead, we have more time for cuddling and canoodling. And we will be alert in the morning, ready to take on the day.

It is your day. Weekends are prime time for sweet pauses, yet household chores often muscle them out. Why give up the best part of the week to life's mundane minutiae? Try to do as many chores as possible during the week with everyone pitching in, or, hire help if you can afford it. Then, consider Saturday or Sunday as a non-negotiable day off. Sleep in, have brunch somewhere funky, and afterwards steal away for a mini-vacation: cycle in the countryside, wander through an art gallery, or fit in a round of golf or a game of tennis. (If small kids are in the picture, hire a sitter, bribe a relative, or trade time off with another couple.) If there are errands still to run, incorporate them into the day in a spirit of fun. If a full day is not possible, put an iron fence around the morning or the afternoon—but *do* pause.

Pause to Ponder
- Can you say what you like best about your partner or special friends?
- How much one-on-one relationship time do you have in a typical week?
- What could you do together if you had more time?
- What keeps you from spending time together? How could you change this?
- What sweet pause could you plan this week? And next?

Walking Wisdom

"Regular walking," said the poet Wordsworth,
"made his life one of unclouded happiness."

"How far is it to the art museum?" I ask Philadelphia tour guide Tish Byrne. "It takes a minute and a half to walk a city block so you're about twenty minutes away," she says. I have the time, so off I go.

What a walk! The air is clear and the weather is light-sweater perfect. Philly folk with smiles as sunny as the day nod hello. History is everywhere. Colonial, Georgian, and neoclassical architecture hold their own against towering glass and steel structures. I pause by the Christ Church Burial Ground to toss a penny on the grave of Benjamin Franklin (a local good-luck tradition) before crossing the street to the Free Quaker Meeting House, a 1783 gem of architectural simplicity. Then I pass the little house where Betsy Ross is said to have sewn the first Stars and Stripes. By the time I reach my destination, I have brushed against the birthplace of America while building a solid bit of exercise into the day.

"I don't spend time in the doctor's office; I walk instead!" says Kit as she buttons up her coat and opens the door. Whether the sky is clear or full of clouds heaving with rain, Kit rambles through her neighborhood, explores a park pathway, or heads to the botanical garden a mile or so away. It will be at least an hour before she returns. "I never miss a day," says this sparkling little lady who is on her way to age ninety. "I have been walking all my life, and I'm not about to stop now!" When asked what draws her to walk, she simply says, "I see more: the scenery, the people, and it makes me feel good, energized."

Walking, that often-mindless motion of putting one foot in front of the other, does much more than get us from A to B. It is good for the body and invites unexpected delights into our day. It opens space for private thoughts and heavenly insights, and frees us from the boxes we live in—boxes that masquerade as houses, offices, cars, and shopping malls. Walking gets us breathing deeply, thinking clearly, and living more soulfully. It is a very pleasurable pause that lets us sense the world around us and gain a measure of solitude, even in a crowded city.

Whether it is a weekend jaunt or a lunchtime escape, walking fosters the ideal union of mind, body, and soul. Now it is being recast as the thing to do. The reason is obvious: almost anyone can do it. We do not need special clothes, training, or expensive facilities, and it is an ideal activity for those who do not consider themselves the sporty type.

We are even taking vacations on the hoof. Where once we sat to tour by car and coach, we now are walking along countryside trails. The devout are making lengthy pilgrimages to holy sites while others are setting lifetime goals of trekking across entire countries (which they might do a section at a time over several years). The Trans Canada Trail, Scotland's West Highland Way, and Switzerland's hut-to-hut trails are filled with students on school breaks and seniors on permanent vacations.

The Best Doctor in Town

Despite the sophistication of contemporary medicine, walking might just be the most effective remedy around. Sir George Trevelyan, the great philosopher and New Age thinker who lived to be ninety years old, is credited with saying, "My two best doctors are my left leg and my right." Today's research supports him.

Perhaps no one has promoted walking for health more than Dr. Yoshiro Hatano of Japan's Kyushu University, who popularized the 10,000 Steps Program to encourage sedentary Japanese to get in shape. The popularity of the program spread to North America, where we usually walk from 3,500 to 5,000 steps daily. Dr. Hatano also is credited with inventing the pedometer, a small device worn on the hip that records each step we take (although Leonardo da Vinci and Thomas Jefferson developed earlier versions). Hatano suggests that walking at a brisk pace (120 steps a minute) for extended distances has significant health benefits. But he admits that 10,000 steps require more than trotting back and forth during our daily routines; we may need to take "intentional walks."

Some of us may plead that our days are already too full: we simply do not have time to wind our watches, let alone count our steps. While that may be true, we can build opportunities into our day if we examine our routines. Walking to the mailbox, getting off the subway a stop early, strolling at lunchtime, and choosing an after-dinner tour around the block instead of an after-dinner drink will put extra steps in the day—and extra days in our life.

Matters of the Heart

The simple act of walking is one of the easiest and cheapest ways to improve the quality and length of our lives. The risk of a stroke during middle age skyrockets for those who sit around. Because coronary heart disease is a leading cause of death in men and women, lacing up a pair of shoes and taking a brisk walk is not a waste of time but an essential, life-enhancing pause from what might seem like more important matters. Walking regularly can cut the risk of heart disease in half, especially in men. British researchers conclude that "couch potatoes" have as high a risk of heart disease as those smokers with elevated levels of cholesterol, or with high blood pressure.[20]

It is startling to note that in 1995 the United Kingdom's Health Education Authority reported that "just under one-third of all coronary heart disease incidence and one-quarter of stroke incidence could be avoided by appropriate exercise."[21] We do not have to speed-walk to benefit. A report for the British Heart Foundation shows that "moderate intensity activity such as walking appears to be at least as effective in reducing blood pressure as more vigorous activity." Best of all, the number of injuries sustained while walking is just about nil, while the positive effect on muscles and bones is without question. A mere hour a week can stimulate positive changes in the body. Doubling that time lowers the risk of type 2 diabetes.

And then there is the question of weight management.

More than half of us are tipping the scales far more than is good for us. The explanation for this can be found in our cushy lifestyles: we drive just about everywhere; our homes are equipped with labor-saving appliances, more of which are invented every year; technology in the workplace has reduced or eliminated many manual tasks and (the popularity of escalators and elevators has left the stairs in the dust); the average Joe or Jane spends the equivalent of nearly a full day each week watching television (more if we include Internet time). Then there is our fast-food, high-calorie diet. All this and more encourages a less active and more sedentary lifestyle.

And it is killing us.

An English study suggests obesity takes seven years off our lives. The older we get, the greater our chances of gaining unwanted weight. The American Obesity Association found that three-quarters of middle-aged women, and an equally disturbing 77 percent of men between sixty-five and seventy-four are overweight. Excess weight puts us at risk of more than thirty medical conditions and increases the likelihood of death from all causes. But there is hope.

Getting out for a stroll can help reduce weight and keep it off. If we commit to a sensible diet and a one-hour walk three days a week, we can lose up to one pound every three weeks. A strenuous up-hill segment within a brisk walk can relieve us of up to fourteen pounds in only three to four months and it can halve the risk of colon cancer (the second most common cancer).

Forever Young

Glowing skin, firm muscles, great posture, and a graceful gait cannot be bought or bottled (at least not yet!). All this and more can be ours by simply walking around the block. Regular walking is a weight-bearing exercise that helps strengthen bones and reduce the risk of osteoporosis and the resulting fractures that affect many post-menopausal women. Those more than forty-five years old will sustain fewer hip fractures because of better balance, co-ordination, and joint flexibility that help to prevent falls.

If we walk in the sunshine, we open ourselves to nature's best source of vitamin D, which is necessary to build strong bones and ward off osteoporosis. Although sunlight has been blacklisted because of its connection with skin diseases, it is a crucial element in reducing the risk of cancers of the breast, prostate, and colon, and of non-Hodgkin's lymphoma. The Canadian Cancer Society indicates that just ten minutes a week will give us what we need (if we forgo the sunscreen). During the summer months, a brief twenty seconds of exposure will aid the body in producing 400 international units of vitamin D, the recommended daily allowance.

Walking is also good news for our gray matter. Lifelong exercise is shown to lessen the chances of developing Alzheimer's disease.[22] Other advantages include an increase in "good" HDL cholesterol and improved stamina and energy.

And that glowing skin? Just pump up a hill or two to get breathing deeply and the blood flowing. Watch stress disappear along with the weight of the world.

Therapy on the Road

One afternoon I was listening to a psychologist on a phone-in radio show. A listener called to say she felt despondent. After a series of questions, I thought the good doctor would recommend antidepressants but she suggested walking every day instead of pill-popping. "If you're new at this," she said gently, "go five minutes in one direction and then come home. Work up to twenty minutes each way."

I do not know how that caller fared, but I was also feeling blue and decided to take the doctor's advice. Out the door I went, even though the couch was calling. I am glad I did. I returned an hour later feeling surprisingly invigorated. I did the same the next day and the next. And now, unless circumstances conspire to prevent it, I anticipate my hour of walking as one of the best pauses in my day.

Links between mental well-being and physical activity stretch back to time immemorial. Even certain clinically depressed subjects have shown improvement when they exercise.[23] Given that 30 percent of women and 20 percent of men will be affected by some form of depression (either directly or through someone close to them), walking for mental health is an easy and pleasant prevention strategy.

Duke University professor Dr. James Blumenthal posits that a brisk, half-hour walk three times a week is as effective in reducing the symptoms of major depression as antidepressant medications. Although researchers do not yet know why this works, some theories suggest that walking increases the release of serotonin and norepinephrine, the same "happy" hormones stimulated by antidepressant medications. Dr. Blumenthal is convinced that although medication may work more rapidly, regular walking may be equally effective and it helps keep symptoms from returning.

Some therapists believe so strongly in the power of walking that they are taking their practice on the road. Dr. John F. Murray, a Florida-based sports psychologist, uses "walking therapy" with nearly 60 percent of his patients. He maintains that many of his patients are more relaxed, think more clearly, and express their feelings more easily when they move. Other psychologists are slowly following his lead.[24]

No one is more convinced of the healing power of walking than Sandra O'Leary. On Wednesdays, she joins a group of other women, rain or shine, for an hour-long Widow's Walk, the most important pause of her week. She started the group in October of 2002 after her husband died. She had looked into organizations that offered a similar programs, but found that they were too bureaucratic.

"Friends and family can only listen so much," Sandra says of why she started the group. "Unless a woman has lost a husband, she can't really understand the hurdles we face. The Widow's Walk gives us a chance to say what we need to say, as often as we need to say it."

"Because we walk in twos, side by side, conversation flows easily. We're not looking each other in the eye. This makes talking about painful issues less intimidating."

The women in her group are aged thirty to eighty-four. Some have been widows for decades, others for weeks. The guidelines for the group are simple: no fees, no unwanted advice, no attendance obligations, and no men. "We've nothing against men," Sandra hastens to add, "but we're not a dating service."

The power of the Widow's Walk is in its silence. "We listen," says Sandra, "and we do not offer advice. When someone needs answers, they'll ask." Sandra explains that, while the focus is on "walking through their grief," the women also share information on where to find a good mechanic or someone to fix the stove, for example. Sandra hopes the idea of the Widow's Walk will spread. She continually welcomes new members by placing a small notice in her local newspaper. "All women need to start their own group is a pair of shoes, ears to hear, and hearts to listen." She offers more information at *www.awidowswalk.ca*.

Walk Talk
Inspire your walk with positive quotes:
- If you want to know if your brain is flabby, feel your legs. — Bruce Barton, U.S. congressman

- All truly great thoughts are conceived while walking. — Friedrich Nietzsche, philosopher
- As you walk down the fairway of life you must smell the roses, for you only get to play one round. — Ben Hogan, golfer
- He that walketh with wise men shall be wise. — Proverbs 13:20
- The man who follows the crowd will usually get no further than the crowd. The man who walks alone is likely to find himself in places no one has been. — Alan Ashley-Pitt, actor
- A pedestrian is a man in danger of his life. A walker is a man in possession of his soul. — David McCord, poet
- Do not be afraid of going slow, be afraid of standing still. — Chinese proverb
- If you have shoes on your feet you can steer yourself in any direction you choose. — Unknown

---

The Friendly Walk

Walking with someone special is a gift we give to each other (assuming both of you turn off your cellphones). It is a testament to the value we place on those we walk with, and it can be darn good fun.

"Walking heightens my sense of discovery, my sense of appreciation for the natural world," says Wendy Bumgardner, who pioneered the popular *walking.about.com* website. "The rhythm of walking integrates body and mind. It leaves my head uncluttered by other intrusions. Even though my weekly route doesn't vary much, I see something new each day. I get in touch with what's around me. It centers me, lets me think through my day, and is my time to pray and receive soulful inspiration."

A couple I know sets aside Saturday mornings for an extended pause, a ritual they began when they married. After a late breakfast, they head out on foot for an adventure. Their destination is a coffee shop where they settle into chairs at an outdoor table (if the weather cooperates) and pour over the weekend crosswords, sip coffee, soak up some sun, and chat about the past week and the one ahead. On their way home, they might stop for a few vegetables or browse through a shop or two. Although seemingly uneventful, it is the time in the week they anticipate more than any other. They arrive home with 10,000 steps under their feet and a few precious hours of completely undistracted time together.

In his book *Man Without a Country*, Kurt Vonnegut shows us just how special walking nowhere in particular can be. I received a story in an e-mail that reflects Vonnegut's sentiments so clearly it is possible that the charming story that follows might also be his.

"I told my wife I was going out to buy an envelope. She said, 'Why don't you go on-line and order ten of them and put them in the drawer.' I pretended not to hear her and out I went to get an envelope because I was going to have one heck of a good time in the process. I met a lot of people, saw some great-looking babes. A fire engine went by and I gave it the thumbs-up. I asked a woman what kind of dog she had and she said 'I don't know.' The moral of the story is we're here on Earth to fart around. Of course, the computer people don't realize or don't care that we are dancing animals. We love to move, but now we're not supposed to dance anymore."

Most of us live in cities buzzing with people, yet we can feel isolated. We have less and less contact with those in our neighborhood and our larger community. Rather than going everywhere by car, how lovely it would be to emulate the old European evening promenade. Little ones could mingle with the older generation and they in turn could share their wisdom. Together we could build an awareness of community, one where people look out for each other and children play safely without fearing the presence of strangers.

Pausing to walk is an essential service we do for ourselves. We feel happier, live healthier, and stay in touch with our inner worlds and with the one around us. It is our best and least expensive medicine, and so easy to take.

Pause to Walk

If you do not have a dog, borrow one. Studies show those responsible for a dog will walk twice as long as those who don't have dogs.[25]

- Try a pedometer. These nifty devices record each step you take and are available at most sports shops. It is motivating to watch your progress
- Keep a journal or graph. Visually recording your daily walk, if only a quick checkmark on the calendar, promotes a sense of accomplishment
- Walk with a purpose. On days you feel like sinking into a sofa, try setting a task within walking distance—such as mailing a letter, buying something special for dinner at the nearby store, or meeting a friend for tea
- Invite a friend to walk with you, or join a club or group. Volkssporters is a worldwide recreational organization for novice and experienced walkers. Check them out at *www.ivv.org* (which links to clubs worldwide)
- Encourage a Neighborhood Walk. A small group on my street has organized the Walky Talkies, when those who feel so inclined go for a stroll

Points to Ponder
- How often do you walk for exercise or just for fun? Daily? Weekly?
- What keeps you from taking a daily stroll? How might you overcome these barriers?
- Where in your day might you fit in a short walk?
- How can you incorporate a longer walk into your weekend or days off work?
- Who might you invite to join you?

Digging in the Dirt

To understand yourself, study a flower.

He dreams of packing away his winter jacket and kicking off his boots to jump into old jeans and sneakers and revel in the garden. Around him he would see plants and pots and spades and a neatly coiled garden hose. Sweet peas would climb up the wall and asters and dahlias would grow beneath them. When it rained he would shoot a prayer heavenwards, grateful for the water that would cool and nourish the neat rows of vegetables and riotous beds of summer blooms. Ah, to be back in the garden with dirt under his nails and sun on his face. When would winter end?

Dirt, glorious dirt! Especially when it is filled with lilies and roses and great bushes of lavender. Whether they be grand estates or humble backyard plots, gardens can be extraordinarily happy places. "Landscapes are a dance, the wind is an orchestra, and the cries of the birds are the high notes in the background," says artist Ted Harrison. "All we have to do is enjoy them."

Our spirit knows the necessity of connecting with nature. We need only hike up to the top of a hill and look over a field to sense the boundless beauty of the natural world. And this does more than refresh the eye: it reminds us of our emotional, spiritual, and physical bond with the Earth. Immersing ourselves in the world of growing things is a sensual, soul-bending pause.

Writer Bruce Wilson suggests nature reminds us that "we are creatures of the Earth, and being part of it puts us in touch with something fundamental to our well-being. Sitting by a wilderness lake, breathing in cool mountain air, and listening to the cry of a loon is much more nourishing than showing off our new SUV or expensively renovated kitchen."

Cultivate a Garden: Cultivate Your Soul

Time passes slowly in the garden. It is a sympathetic diversion from our runaway lives—a gentle, undemanding pause. When we immerse ourselves in a garden, we surrender to its rhythm. Whether we sit in a park or have a green space of our own, a garden teaches us patience. We cannot hurry or control nature: she is in charge, marking time according to her own schedule of growth, bloom, and decay.

I recall a conversation I once had with a woman raised on a sprawling farm. Her parents were avid gardeners. She loved playing among the trees and flowerbeds and eventually she became a skilled and knowledgeable gardener. After she married, she and her husband moved to the city and rented a tiny apartment overlooking a busy street. Its one redeeming feature was a little balcony. Rather than pine for her splendid family home, this resourceful woman gathered together a few old boards and built herself a box. She filled it with soil into which she poked a few seeds, set this on the balcony and, in nature's good time, she had a box brimming with blooms. She was as proud of that little flower box as if it were a grand garden.

Even if it is only a humble box of petunias, pausing to plant and tend a garden, quiets our mental chatter. What a treat to grow fresh herbs, clip fresh basil for a summer salad or a few pungent bay leaves for the soup pot. I have watched a neighbor of mine fuss over his pots of rose bushes for more than five years. When he returns home from the hospital where he works (and often when he's still in his scrubs), out he comes to greet his roses as if they were his children.

Quick-and-Dirty Tips for Container Gardening

I have a friend who grows a variety of vegetables and flowers on her apartment balcony in small containers:

- Wine barrels make ideal containers for herb gardens
- Choose plants non-toxic to people and animals
- Choose containers suitable for fully grown plants.
- Scour the second-hand shops and flea markets for unusual containers that fit your space.
- Consider old wheelbarrows, watering cans, tubs, barrels, or coal buckets for planters—or worn, wooden boards for building them
- Drill drainage holes in container bottoms
- Fill containers with clean soil and compost. Look for pre-mixed soil containing fertilizers
- Depending on what you plant, place in sun or partial shade. Rotate the pots weekly
- Water frequently. Containers will need careful monitoring as they can dry out quickly
- Speak to the experts at the gardening center about which plants are appropriate for the size of your containers. Consider a salad garden of miniature tomatoes, peppers, squash, lettuces,

radishes, and parsley. Herbs such as basil, oregano, and thyme grow well in containers
- Select seasonal flowers such as crocuses, tulips, and daffodils in spring (plant bulbs in the fall), and pansies, alyssum, snapdragons, and marigolds for summer color
- For an instant garden, consider purchasing hanging baskets that are ready-to-hang. Some varieties of strawberries and tomatoes work well in baskets
- Highly fragrant plants such as roses, lavender, and curry provide natural aromatherapy
- Check out books on container gardening for what plants to buy and how to care for them

---

"Gardens ground us, quite literally as well as figuratively," says gardening author Jodi DeLong. "Put your hands into sun-warmed soil, whether to plant bulbs or perennials, vegetables or annuals, trees or shrubs, and you feel a connection with an elemental part of life. Watch a seed thrust its tender but determined green shoots up from the ground into the light and the meaning of life comes into focus."

A garden is a metaphor for hope.

"Whether we believe in science or faith, it's a miracle, pure and simple, that a tiny seed can become a spectacular flower, or food plant, or tree," says Jodi. "It doesn't matter if we are tilling a half-acre vegetable garden, tending a cutting border of flamboyant annual flowers, or caring for a well-loved pot of geraniums on a sunny window ledge: the effects of gardening on our well-being are infinite and wonderful."

For some, getting a "green fix" is as easy as climbing onto a roof. A worldwide initiative is afoot to build rooftop gardens. While the concept is not new, the idea is making a comeback in modern-day architecture. Canada, America, India, and China have joined other countries in adopting rooftop gardens as a solution for storm-water retention. "Green roofs also provide excellent insulation," says architect Terrence Williams, a leader in environmental design. "They help cool the environment and significantly reduce noise."

They also provide a green oasis in our steel-and-concrete cities. Williams tells of visiting Brit's Pub in Minneapolis, where he was invited upstairs to visit a bowling green. There he discovered the English Garden Park, an 18,000-square-foot rooftop garden with forty-two tables, a small bar, and a kitchen. Built among the trees and manicured flowerbeds were 10,000 square feet of bowling greens. "The place was packed," he says. As the owners, Shane and Stuart Higgins, boast, "There's no better place to tip a pint and play with your bowls!" While a bowling green over a pub is not everyone's idea of a garden experience, the idea of repurposing these spaces opens the door for city dwellers to create natural settings within their neighborhoods.

Natural Healing

"The garden reflects the face of the divine and the quest for a return to paradise," wrote Helen Chesnut in her regular *Victoria Times Colonist* column. "Creating and maintaining a garden is, in a sense, an exercise in reclaiming Eden. Here, we become co-creators with God and cultivators of life. In some mysterious way, we cleanse, soothe, and cultivate our minds and souls as we plant and tend our gardens."

While the connection between the natural environment and humans is certainly intuitive, University of Michigan psychologists Rachel Kaplan and Stephan Kaplan confirm that when people spend even short periods in natural settings they feel calmer and more at peace with themselves. They also found that we are happier and more productive if we have even a minimal view of bushes, trees, or a lawn. If we do not have the corner office, we can still benefit from a vicarious pause with nature by just looking at a picture of a landscape.

Roger Ulrich, the director of the Texas A&M Center of Health Systems and Design, noticed that patients with window views had shorter hospital stays and fewer complications than those who faced blank walls. I reached a similar conclusion when my brother spent several weeks bed-ridden in hospital. He constantly remarked on the view from his window of the distant hills. Then he was moved to another unit with enclosed walls. He became agitated, irritable, and had difficulty sleeping.

When he was well enough to be discharged, he asked to visit a beach near his home. There he sat in his wheelchair contemplating the ocean, islands, and distant mountains he had seen countless times before his illness. He continued going every day. "I don't know if it's spiritual or what, but something pulls me here," he said. "I know it sounds clichéd, but it's tranquil. I can think things through and whatever the weather, I can't have a bad experience."

Although my brother had been told he was unlikely to walk again, within a short while he was slowly making his way along the esplanade on foot. While many factors may have contributed to his remarkable recovery, I felt he was experiencing natural healing at its finest.

Like an ocean breeze that bathes us in the scent of the sea, pausing to immerse ourselves in nature's embrace is an act of kindness we do for ourselves. It is then that we can slow down and connect with goodness and beauty. It is then that we can feel the heartbeat of the Earth. Whether we sink our hands into the soil, admire a hilltop vista, toss a lawn bowl on a rooftop green, or pick a few sage leaves for the teapot, romping in the sweet world of nature is a release from the runaway life, a pause worth planting.

Pause to Ponder

- Choose a quiet spot outdoors and recall a pleasant interlude you have had in nature. Remember how you felt then. What smells do you associate with this experience? What emotions does it evoke?
- Take an inventory of your work and living spaces. What elements of nature do they include?
- How can you make additions that will enhance your personal nature connection in these spaces? Think about adding plants or reassigning space.
- What natural settings are within walking distance of your home or workplace?
- Commit to spending even a few minutes each day in one of these spaces. Taking a bag lunch to a park is an ideal way to give your spirit and body a midday renewal.

Backyard Adventure

*If we pause and really look, familiar places
offer defining moments.*

*"Y'all know what a pick-up is?" our fly-fishing guide Rick
asks Mary, Dawn, and me with a mischievous grin. My friends,
who are having a mini-vacation just down the road from where
they live, return questioning looks. With that, Rick raises his rod
and lets go a perfectly cast fly that settles ever so lightly upon the
river. "That's not my kind of pickup," says Mary, thinking of her
truck sitting in the driveway. "Nor mine," adds Dawn with a
naughty nod in the direction of a hard-bodied fly fisher casting
downstream. While we might disagree on what a "pick-up"
means, we do learn the difference between a pole and a rod. "If it
costs under a hundred dollars, it's a pole," chuckles Rick.*

Even if we go no farther than the end of the street, an
adventurous pause opens us to the rhythm of a place, lets
us touch its nuances, and delve into its mysteries. It takes
us off our beaten track and allows us to reassess our priorities and renew our relationship with ourselves, and those
who might come with us. If we move at a slow, deliberate

pace, our awareness of sights and smells around us will be heightened.

I have had the great fortune to venture abroad, a perk of my role as a speaker and writer. But wherever I go, I return home with a deeper affection for where I live. It is an odd irony that traveling often makes us see our own backyard with fresh eyes. It makes us realize that, if we take the time and pause, we may discover treasures right down the road.

Playing in our own stomping ground is an adventure that lets us have fun and still be home for dinner. It takes the familiar and spins it around, allowing us to see it from the inside out, and upside down, one little journey at a time. We can escape in the lunch hour or make a weekend of it. Checking out our own backyard is a pause that pushes aside our obligations and commitments, a mini-vacation that can be loaded with those unexpected delights that give life a boost (and is easy on the wallet).

Trolley buses and carriage rides are not just for tourists. Pausing to appreciate the cultural treasures in the overlooked nooks and crannies down the street gives us a sense of place, a feeling of continuity, and, if nothing else, a small diversion from the day's pressures.

Put on squeaky-clean sneakers and a cheesy T-shirt, toss a camera around your neck, and get ready to play tourist. Hop on the sightseeing buses. Horse-drawn carriage rides are fun. Ride the gondolas, take the garden tours, and visit the historic houses the city fathers built. Discovering the stories behind the statues in the park and the person to whom a public fountain is dedicated puts the past on our map.

Summon your inner sleuth. Adventures, stories, and intrigues are lurking in alleyways and hiding behind the facades of the most nondescript buildings. Tourist bureaus often help to arrange walking or bus tours, even for the locals.

If research is your thing, plan an afternoon in the local archives. Old newspapers, photographs, letters, books, paintings, census reports, stories of prominent citizens now long-departed, and other remnants of the past can lead to fascinating discoveries. Perhaps a famous battle was fought on the hill behind the old factory. Main Street might once have been a trail used by rum-runners during Prohibition. Such local lore gives depth to where we live. It is great fun to wander down a well-known street with an old map in hand (obtain a copy from the archives) and discover who lived where and what has changed. If we are very lucky, we just might run into an old-timer or local historian who will sit awhile and share their stories.

Pausing among the painters lets us brush up against greatness, and often it's free. Don Monet, a painter and owner of Cube, an art gallery in Ottawa, says those who amble into his shop act nothing like the busybodies on the street outside. "Galleries are like churches. There is a sense of awe. People become quiet. They sit, rest, and take time." English psychologist Angela Chow determined that we do indeed de-stress when rambling among oils, pastels, and watercolors. She and her team found harried workers in London's financial district felt more relaxed after an hour in a gallery and that their levels of cortisone, a stress-related hormone that causes wear and tear in the body, dropped significantly.

Whether public or private, galleries express the unique character and features of a community. The C.M Russell Museum in Great Falls, Montana, for example, is filled with grand paintings and bronze sculptures depicting the heartache and romance of the dying days of the Wild West. In Halifax, the Art Gallery of Nova Scotia has enshrined the work of folk artist Maud Lewis, a tiny lady who captured her simple rural life on every surface of the wee cabin she shared with her husband Everett. After her death in 1970, their little home was installed en masse inside the gallery, a wonderful tribute to the artist and a fascinating work of art for all to enjoy.

I do hope the good people of Philadelphia take time to appreciate *The Dream Garden*, a remarkable mural that dominates the foyer of the Curtis Center in the city's historic area. Based on a painting by Maxfield Parrish and created in 1916 by Louis Tiffany, this masterpiece is fashioned from 100,000 pieces of colored glass. When seen from a distance, the scene of valleys, waterfalls, mountains, and streams resembles a painting. It is a spectacular expression of whimsy and open to anyone who takes a few minutes to venture inside the building.

Playing among the dearly departed can be a soulful pause. Cemeteries are losing their reputation as ghoulish places and becoming sought-after places to pause. Houses situated across from these quiet spots are rising in value and commanding top dollar in some cities. There is, after all, little chance the neighbors will be rowdy.

Local history is an open book if you tap into the spirit of Sherlock Holmes and study the mortuary stones of old cemeteries. These cryptic records can reveal fascinating stories of a community's history. Many gravestones raise questions, and we can enjoy finding (or making up!) the answers.

Take a book walk. If we have a penchant for travel stories, mysteries, crime fiction, or spiritual inspiration, then spending an afternoon in a bookstore can be an intriguing pause. I am irresistibly attracted to the stacks of used books in the shops along the main street of Sidney, an enchanting seaside village on the island where I live. In shops like these, we might find British mysteries stacked from floor to ceiling or nautical tales crowding the shelves. Perhaps leather-bound editions of Browning, Keats, and Yeats dominate the space. And there are romantic tales of Siam and Persia and Arabia. I can spend hours rummaging through the shelves and often find a little gem. I leave feeling as if I had taken a trip—perhaps I have.

Discovering what authors say about where we live can give us a fresh perspective on our hometown. We might pore over the guidebooks with their detailed descriptions of places to see and things to do, or read travel narratives set in our neck of the woods. Researching our town as if it were a foreign destination can be the beginning of unusual discoveries and adventures.

The ancient village of Hay-on-Wye in Wales is a bibliophile's heaven where more than forty bookstores line the old streets. Each spring, the village of 1,500 residents hosts one of the largest literary festivals in the world.

There are times when it is okay to play with your food, whatever your mother might have told you, especially when noshing on the local specialties. This means po-boys in New Orleans, cheesesteaks in Philly, and fish chowder in Lunenburg. My husband Bob and I are keen on rich, dark ale brewed in a pub not far from where we live. Sometimes we have lunch at a little place with mouth-puckering lemon tarts and then roam a street cluttered with eclectic shops where vintage clothing, second-hand furniture, and tacky posters tempt passersby. Afterward, we might pick up fresh vegetables and barbecued pork from Chinatown before heading home.

Armchair traveling is also a playful pause. While some of us will pack a lunch and head out the door, others will make unforgettable journeys without leaving the living room. We can trek through Australia's parched outback, prance along flawless beaches, and watch the sun bake Ayers Rock into a shimmering haze. We can even down a pint in a Darwin pub. All we need to do is visit the library, pick up a copy of Bill Bryson's *In a Sunburned Country*, and settle into a comfy chair. Travel writers like Bryson bring adventures to us. We do not have to queue at the airport, struggle with luggage, or attempt our dinner choices in unfamiliar languages; we just have to pause long enough to turn the pages.

H.V. Morton, one of the best-loved travel writers of the twentieth century, can bring the soul of Britain right into our living room.[26] Little does it matter that some of his most fascinating chronicles were written more than seventy years ago. Like all good writers that transport us into their experiences, Morton's poetical descriptions, critical observations, and sense of humor can jet the armchair traveler into the remote Scottish Highlands, down into the dungeons of a Welsh castle, and through the lively streets of London.

Whether fly-fishing on a river or shopping in an open-air market, we bring adventure in when we venture out. Looking beyond our back door opens us up to a life with unpredictable possibilities. It replaces daily routines with new agendas and new challenges. While these sojourns might not be the stuff of great epics, we can fit them in on the way home from work, in an afternoon, or on a weekend. These are the pauses that put fun in the week, and a twinkle in our lives.

Tips for Backyard Adventures
- Pick up a walking map and plan a day hoofing around town
- Visit the archives to research the history of your neighborhood
- Spend an hour in a gallery
- Take an afternoon and check out the museums
- Take a tour of the town marketed to tourists
- Visit tourist attractions, one by one
- Check out the new restaurants, bite into the street food (and try a glass of the local brew)

Pause to Ponder
- When did you last go sightseeing in your home town?
- What attractions do you recommend to visitors?
- How well do you know your local history?
- What backyard adventure could you plan for an afternoon or a full day?

Small Indulgences

Small pleasures let us step back from the pressures of the day, if only for a few moments.

The late afternoon sun is still warm when she packs up her briefcase and strolls down the street to the old part of town. She sits at a table outside a little deli where unruly bushes of rosemary and lavender escape from oversized pots, and baskets of geraniums hang heavy under the eaves. She breathes deeply. Oh, life is good.

When she has settled into this cocoon of growing things, she orders a cup of tea and sits, thinking of nothing at all. After she drains the last drop, she wanders into a little bookstore. There she peruses the titles and chooses one about adventures in the Australian outback. When she leaves for home, she feels content that mind, body, and soul have been pleasantly satisfied. Small indulgences. Small pleasures. A perfect after-work pause.

In 1991, Faith Popcorn, a trend-spotting guru who advises Fortune 500 companies, predicted we would gravitate towards high-quality but affordable treats to take the edge off our increasingly uncertain and complex world. How right she was! A pause to indulge in little luxuries puts a splash of pleasure in our lives. It is a recess from the happenings of the day and provides a buffer between work and home—a breathing space without demands. Making time for small pleasures is an act of spiritual maintenance, a kindness we do for ourselves.

Faith stressed that small indulgences do not have to cost a pocketful of money. Instead of ordering a new wardrobe, we can settle for a shirt. We can pass on the five-star restaurant for something less pretentious but no less delightful— say a cup of mint-and-jasmine tea—exotic and refreshing with a healthy dose of glamour. When we sip a sinful latte, nibble a decadent Belgium chocolate, or sport a new handrolled tie, we feel special and a wee bit spoiled.

Tom, a tough-minded lawyer working with a busy city firm, has a ritual he shared with me. Every Monday on his way to work, he stops by a bakery for a still warm cinnamon bun and coffee. "It sets up the week," he says with a grin. "They've got the best buns in town, all gooey and covered in nuts."

Carmen and her daughter Nicole, who operate a little deli and cheese shop, say that little treats bring back good memories. "Certain tastes, or the way a specialty item is made, can remind us of life's high points," says Carmen, who emigrated from Holland. On her shelves she stocks fig preserves from Croatia's Dalmatian coast and grainy mustard from the Netherlands. Her cheeses come from France, Germany, and England. A visit to her shop is a trip back to the old country and her customers don't even have to buy a ticket. This queen of small indulgences is not immune to the wonderful specialties she offers others. "If I were back in Holland, I'd be sitting at one of the outdoor cafés with a wonderful cup of coffee topped with whipped cream and a delicious pastry, so, instead, I whip myself up a cup and think of home."

Think of artisan-baked bread, scented soap made just down the road, or a hand-knit scarf. None of these items will break the bank, but each makes us feel grand, which is the whole point of the exercise.

The Perfect Small Indulgence Should Be ...

Tantalizing—creates a feeling of excitement with a
   touch of impatience
Ego-satisfying—makes us feel special
Affordable—will not leave a dent in our wallet
A bright spot in a dull day—gives momentary
   pleasure with long-lasting memories
Handmade—improves the mix
Custom-made—feels even better

Sandy, an office manager in an isolated northern Alberta community, has mastered the art of spoiling herself. "After a long, hard run on a cold winter day, even before I take a shower, I put on my fleece pajamas, curl up on the couch with a big blanket, and watch movies. It takes me back to my childhood. Another pleasure of mine (keep in mind I live in the Great White Canadian North) is sitting before a roaring fire and sipping a great glass of wine."

Dave likes to chill out with a pint of English bitter. It reminds him of where he grew up, and as he says, "It tastes particularly good when I watch a soccer match on the telly."

Whether on the weekend or squeezed into the workday, we can spoil ourselves with a playful pause in countless ways. It is fun to make a list and then work through it, one pleasurable moment at a time. Here are suggestions from some friends:

- Books, beers, bikes, skis, friends...and the time to enjoy them.   Robert in Calgary

- Chocolate, sex, and watching really stupid comedies. Tanya in Toronto
- My idea of bliss is to get my husband out of the house, run a bath, set up a little table beside the tub, and relax in the warm bubbles with a hot cup of tea and a Harlequin novel for an hour or more. Not very original, I'm afraid, but it is amazing just how seldom I actually get to do this. Debbie in Prince Edward Island
- Get a massage. Kathleen in Montreal
- I play shakuhachi [a bamboo flute], trim the bonsai, and admire the chickadees darting deftly between the branches. Bruce in Montreal
- Taking a few hours to myself so I can write creatively, perhaps pen a few poems without interruptions. Lorraine in Kelowna
- Grab the odd piece of chocolate, listen to some great jazz, or just go out for a run. Leslie in Edmonton
- Turn the phone off and relax with a good novel and a big bowl of fresh, hot, buttered popcorn...yummy! Pat in Arizona

Small indulgences can be as satisfying as taking a vacation, and we can enjoy them more often. They sweeten the edge of a tough day and put a little luxe into life. A special coffee, fresh flowers for the dinner table, or homemade jam with toast before we head off to work are mini-treats that confirm we are top-notch. The more we appreciate ourselves, the more life shines. Pausing to pursue small pleasures is not the solution to all life's challenges, but it does give the day a jolt of joy, instantly.

Indulgences That Won't Break the Bank
- Top-quality golf balls
- Pedicures (this is great for the guys, too)
- Handmade soap
- Freshly baked cinnamon buns
- A specialty beer in a quiet pub
- A new gardening tool
- Organic toothpaste
- Imported jam
- Freshly made pasta from the deli
- The bestseller everyone's talking about
- Long lunches with friends
- Bath stuff that smells great
- A new cookbook
- Funny weekend socks
- Beautifully designed journaling books
- Great cheeses
- Smoked salmon on pumpernickel bread
- Late-night jazz and a fine bottle of wine

Pause to Ponder
- What is your favorite small indulgence?
- When did you last treat yourself to something small but truly wonderful?
- What small indulgence might you share with a special person in your life?
- How could you surprise a stranger with a special treat?
- What three small indulgences could you enjoy in the coming month?
- What could you do to treat yourself each day?

Spa-ed Rotten

Perhaps the sin is not *pampering yourself!*

I am at a day spa for a posh pause, a gift from my husband. A very pretty woman with a china-doll face hands me a fluffy robe and a steaming cup of tea. She shows me into a dressing area that is decorated with the colors of sand and earth and sky. Sounds of the pan flute float through the hushed room as I peruse the menu of body wraps, exfoliations, massages, hydrotherapy, facials, and pedicures. Hmm, I think, this is downright wonderful.

I liked slopping in mud as a kid, so I settle on a mud wrap, under the illusion I would be on somewhat familiar ground. Then the fun begins. After an invigorating skin exfoliation, out comes the warmed, organic mud for a thorough lathering. After that, I spend thirty minutes wrapped in a heated blanket, floating in a surreal world of trance-inducing music, soft light, and orange-blossom scent. After a brisk shower, I am back on Earth feeling rejuvenated yet tranquil from the inside out, and absolutely spa-ed rotten.

An escape to a day spa can be a very self-indulgent pause—a reward for finishing grad school, getting a promotion, or just because we want to de-stress and rejuvenate. We can stay for an hour or make a day of it. If we have the time and the funds, we can head off to a resort spa for a couple of days. Whatever we choose, we will leave the runaway life behind us when we put ourselves in the soothing hands of the masseuse and nestle into the seductive sounds and smells of these womb-like retreats.

Massage and other "body work" not only feels terrific, it releases the tension held in our muscles, and it revitalizes, detoxifies, and energizes us while soothing our inner beast. For those of us who work at computers, have high-stress, demanding jobs, or are responsible for the care of others, taking time to spoil ourselves is not selfish, but smart and prudent. Self-care fills our inner well with the emotional and spiritual vitality. While it might seem self-indulgent, it is an essential, as well as playful, pause.

Spas are not just for the rich and famous. A little creative budgeting and careful scrutiny of our spending habits may free up enough cash for the occasional hands-on experience. From the California coast to the seductive shores of Thailand, brawny construction workers, businessmen, alpha guys and gals, and matrons in sensible shoes are lining up with the ladies who lunch to get pummeled and pampered.

While the spa craze might seem like the latest hot trend, it has been around since the townspeople in Merano, Italy, began dipping into their natural mineral baths before Caesar ran Rome. Hot tubs existed in Egypt as early as 600 BC, and when the Turks, Romans, and Greeks weren't conquering new lands, they were soaking their saddle sores in steamy cauldrons. More than a millennium later, Queen Elizabeth I insisted on "taking the baths" at least once a month.

And where else can you get thoroughly (and legally) stoned? Hot stone massage dates back 2,000 years and is again attracting followers. Therapists use smooth basalt rocks heated to 115 F to knead, caress, and coax tension from sore muscles and stiff joints. With aromatherapy massage, clients sniff their way through a choice of essential oils before choosing their preference for a full-body work-over. "Both these treatments have a spiritual significance for those who feel a special connection with the Earth's elements," says massage specialist Doreen Home.

For centuries, Japanese families have ended the day soaking in the *ofuro*, a freestanding tub filled with steamy water. The custom was imported to North America after World War II, when a few crafty Californians converted oak casks, wine tanks, and olive vats from nearby wineries into hot tubs.

We have come a long way since reclining in recycled Cabernet barrels. Today's experiences are intriguing and exotic. The list of spa-menu items offers a round-the-world experience: Dead Sea mud masks, Himalayan wraps, Swedish massage, Merlot soaks, massages with honey and Hawaiian macadamia nut oil, and West Coast seaweed facials. (I must admit I have wondered if mud from the Dead Sea, the Colorado River, or the frigid shores of Baffin Island really has it over good old backyard muck. And I am not sure about letting it all hang out in a tub of wine. But it is fun thinking about lathering one's body in something you can't get at the corner store.)

A spa experience can really punch up our life, but it can be somewhat intimidating for the first-timer. "Stripping down is the spa newbie's number one concern," says Doreen, who has seen it all in her many years in the spa business. "A person's privacy is protected at all times.

Therapists drape sheets and towels discreetly over the body. Some clients keep on their underwear. People don't know what to expect, but they're in charge. We don't see anything they don't want to show us, although Europeans, who are often regular spa-goers, just peel off their clothes and hop on the table," she adds with a giggle.

Women have eagerly jumped on the spa wagon, and guys are also booking appointments. Wanting to entice my husband (then a spa virgin) into the spa experience, I arranged for him to try a neck massage and a pedicure. "I was okay starting with something safe. And boy, was it great," he admits. "What they did to these pegs of mine was amazing and that massage was the best feeling in the world—well, almost," he adds with an impish grin. "I'm sneaking back even if the guys think I'm a wuss."

Recipe for a Do-it-yourself Posh Pause

While stepping into the magical realm of the professional spa is a heady experience, we can also create our own wonder world at home.

The Elements
- An uncluttered room: give the space you plan to use (usually a bathroom) a thorough cleaning and remove distracting items from the counters, shelves, and walls to give the room a quiet, Zen-like simplicity
- Water: purchase or borrow a small water feature to provide the background sound of a waterfall. You'll also need a tub of warm bath water to soak in, and a small basin if you want to soak your feet
- Music: forget hip hop; choose soft, slow music

- Silence: aside from music, turn off the radio, television, and please, no cellphones
- Scent: fill your room with fresh, strongly scented flowers such as carnations, roses, freesias or lilies, or put essential oils in the bathwater
- Candles: little tea candles emit an exotic glow
- Products: visit the beauty counter of a bath or department store. Treat yourself to fragrant soaps, body oils, or lotions. Try a facial treatment and body exfoliation

The Experience
- Set aside enough time to enjoy your spa and a follow-up nap
- Fill your tub, turn on the music, light the candles, and let yourself be spa-ed rotten
- Read, daydream, or let your thoughts wander

Gone Fishin'

Sometimes getting spa-ed rotten means skipping town. Irene, who co-manages a small family business and helps raise five young grandchildren, does just this. Although she's a busy lady, this did not stop her from joining five of her cousins for a seven-day cruise. Each morning she luxuriated in the ship's spa, where she soaked in the hydro-pool to subdue her stress. "Pure heaven, it was," she says. "That week was all about me. I was thoroughly, totally pampered. As for the cost? I figured it was less than a latte a day [calculated over a year], which I can afford because getting away from my everyday life is a sanity-saver."

As for feeling guilty? She admits to a nagging feeling that she was abandoning her post but, as she put it, "everyone managed just fine while I was away."

Irene continues, "I want my life to be a collection of wonderful experiences, whether it is enjoying the unfolding of an amaryllis bloom, taking a day trip, or vacationing for a week to rest my body and renew my spirit. Creating different, enriching experiences keeps me sane. A vacation by myself, or with family or friends, refreshes my outlook on life. I have done all three. A very memorable time was spent aboard a schooner in the Queen Charlotte Islands. I went by myself but quickly became friends with the other passengers. That getaway so enriched my life that I still savor the experience, and it was—my goodness—seventeen years ago. It doesn't take piles of money. Putting aside a little each day (I brown-bag my lunch) is enough to spoil myself rotten at least once a year."

Getting spoiled rotten is not just about tripping down to a spa. Each summer, Harald joins a group of twenty men for a week of fishing. They live in simple barrack-style accommodations and make their own meals. He has been part of this group for the past several years. "It is a total break, instant relaxation," says the building contractor. "The camaraderie is great. I'd do it several times a year if I could."

Harald speaks of his passion for the outdoors that he developed as a child. While he likes to escape on his fishing expeditions, he also steals away into the backcountry several weekends each summer with his partner Sue. "We get instant peace. For twenty bucks a night we can park our camper at the edge of a lake with a million-dollar view," says Sue. She sums up their experience by saying, "No phone, no fence to paint or weeds to pull. No chores, no cares."

The idea of spoiling ourselves, even just a little, might seem like a sin of sorts. This, I think, is a crying shame. The occasional personal pause boosts our feel-good factor and polishes up the soul. While taking a cruise or camping by the lakeside is not everyone's idea of a getaway, if we give it some thought we'll discover the way we like to be pampered. Doing this keeps us ready and able to handle life's bumps and bruises. A very important pause, wouldn't you agree?

Pause to Ponder
- When did you last do something totally for yourself?
- What holds you back?
- What would be your ideal posh pause?
- How can you make this happen?
- If money is an issue, how can you adapt a posh pause to fit your budget?

Welcome Home ...

to your perfect place to pause

How often have we hungered for a refuge from the outside world when the workday is done? Somewhere that is intensely personal, comforting, and calm. Our soul needs a place of retreat, its very own personal paradise, a place where we set down our load and put up our feet, a place that radiates with the warmth of the familiar and is anchored by what matters to us most. We may have little control over what happens beyond our front door, but we can influence the ambience inside our home.

The four chapters in this section provide suggestions to transform your home into a perfect place to pause. They will examine why:

- Purging our homes of physical clutter eliminates mental distractions and opens space to live and love and *just be*
- Organizing possessions so they are at hand ensures tranquility not turmoil
- Creating a healthy, clean environment lets us re-energize in a home that is sensually pleasing
- Transforming our homes into personal sanctuaries make them perfect places to pause

Pause to Purge

Attachments to old stuff keep us from new pleasures.

The afternoon sun filters into the small room and dances around the scent of lilac. A sofa and two worn chairs frame a carpet of burgundy, gold, and blue. Above the fireplace hangs a painting of the Scottish Highlands awash in blooming heather. A book rests on a burl table, a fine piece from Holland bought second-hand from a neighbor. Every table, book, and picture expresses the life journeys of the people who live here. What a joy to sit or read here, or to tuck into a corner and snooze. The room is a retreat for the soul—a refuge for repose and for renewal.

It is said that Queen Victoria's favourite refuge was not one of her many castles, but a simple peasant cottage. On visiting the wilds of Scotland, she was charmed by a plain, sparse shepherd's hut. Victoria wrote that its "feelings of goodwill" so impressed her that she and Prince Albert often stayed there. As that great lady did, so do we all need a place to feel truly at home.

A perfect place to pause supports our current journey and honors the paths we have trodden. Whether it is humble or grand, it draws us in and holds us safe. It is as comforting as old slippers and a place where we can laugh and dream and, when the dark days of winter set in, find shelter for our body and our soul.

My uncle's prairie farmhouse, which served the family through three generations, was such a place. Everything about it said "home," especially the enormous kitchen. I remember well the old sofa with its deep, comfy cushions and the rocking chair that my cousins and I would squeeze into when we were kids. In the center of the kitchen was an oak table large enough for the extended family to crowd around, and where, at harvest time, an entire threshing crew could hunker down over mashed potatoes and fried chicken.

On the wall hung a calendar with pictures of winter landscapes, newborn lambs, and gardens in full bloom. Family pictures rested on the walnut cabinet where my aunt kept her precious ornaments and the good china. On cool autumn days the smell of apple and wild berry pies wafted from the old coal-and-wood stove that kept the room warm no matter how fierce the wind. Everything in the room had purpose. This was a place to work, think, relax, laugh, and pause.

Stuffed to Death

When I conduct seminars, I often ask audiences to close their eyes and think of a room that makes them feel safe and content. As they do this, I can see them relax. Some even smile. Then I ask them to visualize themselves in a room they do not like, or one they avoid. Facial expressions dramatically change. Rather than being open and soft, faces become tense and tight. When I ask what they experienced during the second part of that exercise, some will express feelings of anxiety, guilt, depression, confusion, and a sense of being overwhelmed. When I ask why, the answer is often the same: *too much stuff.*

Our living environment is our kingdom, whether it's a mansion with a spectacular view, or a bedsit in a house we share with others. It is where we retreat from the hurly-burly of the outside world. Yet, frequently our serene sanctuaries are depots for clutter. It is no wonder: when we unwind, it is too often behind a shopping cart. Shopping ranks just behind television as our preferred way to spend our leisure time. Even though we continue to buy, most of us use only 20 percent of what we have (these tend to be things that support our current lifestyle) while legions of "freeloaders" pack corners and cabinets, or hide away in closets, attics, and storage rooms. There they squat, sometimes for decades.

The author Bill West, an expert in garage reorganization, feels clutter can easily take over our lives: "Garage remodeling and organizing is a new category in home improvement that gives a fresh perspective to the largest and most abused room in our homes," he says. He emphasizes that 83 percent of North American homes built in 2004 are designed for two- or three-car garages, but this space becomes the family dump, protecting heaps of stuff we do not use while cars worth thousands of dollars sit in the driveway.

"Cluttered garages are a growing problem, with North Americans spending more than $800 million annually on products designed for organizing garages. The easiest solution is to let go of what we do not need and allocate the money for something fun." That means the bikes and camping gear stay, but the unpacked boxes from the last move go.

Many of us have areas in our homes where we feel more comfortable than others. It is interesting to consider why such spaces have this effect on us. It is possible that we avoid sorting the cluttered areas because they contain unfinished projects or reminders of unhappy times. We *see* unanswered mail, but *feel* guilt. Kitchen counters awash in dirty dishes, unanswered telephone messages, fridges full of jars of this and tubs of that, might make us feel like inept slobs. Physically purging objects that stir negative feelings psychically eliminates mental and emotional sludge and liberates space for more positive purposes.

You Are What You Own

Examining things we have lived with can be illuminating, especially if they have been part of our surroundings for many years, for they often contain messages about who we are. Let's examine a bookshelf. What stories does it tell? Are we curious, romantic, adventurous, nostalgic, politically inclined, escapist, or fascinated with erotica? Have our tastes changed or remained consistent? Are we off in new directions? Do art or travel books compete for space with a mystery series? Are there multiple copies of the same title? Is the bookshelf a store of remembrances of childhood? Are there volumes we reread, like to hold, or simply look at? Why? And what if there are books we dislike yet feel obliged to keep? Are we bunged up with remnants from the past? Perhaps we are piling new on top of old, instead of letting life pass gracefully through and around us.

All these questions come to mind when we pause to remove things we own from their shelves or closets, clean the space, and then—one by one—choose whether or not to replace them. This process lets us reassess what is still relevant and may lead us to unload some of our possessions for others to enjoy. This in-and-out creates a flow that clears space for new ideas and new possessions.

Whether it is books, clothes in the closet, or boxes in the attic, taking time to contemplate what our stuff says about our personal journey can offer insight into who we are, where we have been, what matters, and what does not. Taking such an inventory lets us assess whether the things we own still serve or inspire us while enabling us to purge others that we may not use, have duplicates of, or that trigger negative feelings.

Taking Back the Garage

Start on one side of the room with several large boxes. Have plenty of garbage bags on hand. Examine every item and classify it as a keeper, a candidate for charity or a yard sale, or garbage. Be ruthless. If you can't immediately decide, ask these questions: Why am I keeping this? Will I ever use this? If so, when?

When the clutter is gone, sort what is left into logical storage categories such as tools, gardening supplies, sports equipment, and automotive supplies. Put out-of-season sports equipment out of reach, leaving accessible space for items in current use. Garage walls offer prime storage space. Invest in a wall-mounted grid to hold shelves, hooks, and bins, and a set of drawers for smaller items. A rolling mechanic's toolbox is ideal for storing tools, as is a folding workbench. An excellent book on organizing garages is Bill West's *Your Garagenous Zone: Innovative Ideas for the Garage.*

My Junk, Your Treasure

Eliminating clutter culprits—those things that do not serve us practically, emotionally, or spiritually—gives us more space and a more restful environment as well as a healthy dollop of feel-good. When we clear our clutter, we clear our heads. Rooms filled with too much stuff are not the rooms that invite us in. Instead of enticing us to put up our feet, they send us bolting out the door. A wonderful guideline was left to us by the British socialist, craftsman and writer William Morris: "have nothing in your houses that you do not know to be useful or believe to be beautiful."

The uncluttered room, like the uncluttered life, differentiates between *wants* and *needs*. His Holiness the Dalai Lama shows us the difference. This master of diplomacy is frequently given gifts that he graciously accepts, but he would be awash in stuff if he kept them all. I have seen him warmly express his appreciation and then, if the item does not further his goals of peace and service to others, hand it off, not later, but immediately so it can be sent to someone who needs it. A gift is a symbol of the intention of the giver. That is where the value is.

Just imagine the good our unused things could do, the relief we would feel, and the space we would liberate if we followed His Holiness's example and replaced hoarding with generosity. Tanya, who was preparing to move, put the Dalai Lama's example into action. Here is the note she sent me:

Here's what I've accomplished so far:
- Two large bags of novels donated to family
- Three boxes of books donated to charity
- Two bags of teddy bears donated to charity

- Equivalent of three boxes of various items donated to the drop-in center near my office, including lotions, shampoos, etc. that never get used
- Expired medication discarded
- Getting rid of kitchen stuff, etc.
- A couple of bags of clothes
- Probably a computer to go now, too
- And massive amounts of junk paper

I asked Tanya how her house felt as she moved her stuff along. "It feels emptier, but not empty. I still have some knickknacks that have strong memories, but I realize I don't need ten souvenirs of the same trip to recreate it."

She also replied that is was "really something to see what my stuff meant to other people. At one point I had more than 300 stuffed bears. I have gradually been discarding them but still had close to 100 different types, some stuffed, some wood, some ceramic, glass, and so on.

"I donated two bags to college students who were collecting them for kids (but kept the bear I got when I was born, and Elmo and Tigger). I also took a couple of boxes to the drop-in center next to where I work. It turns out that one woman who comes here loves teddy bears and was so excited to have some...well...all of them. As hard as it was to make a break with this collection, seeing someone so over the moon about those bears made it that much easier. One person's junk really.is another's treasure."

It took Sam just a few minutes to clear a box of books from the shelves of the room he had designated to be his personal "place to pause." Many had been there for decades, a record of his interior journey. After a moment of hesitation, he started tossing paperbacks into the box. Out went Grisham. Then McCourt, Cornwell, and Fowles followed, as did books he had not opened since college. When the box was full he put it by the back door. Sam was expecting visitors that afternoon and they would be invited to have their pick. "It feels good," he says. "Books come into my life so easily. Now I'm reversing the flow."

Over several weeks, Sam continued clearing his shelves, keeping only those books that he felt deserved repeated readings. When he had finished purging his library, he used the free space to display a collection of photographs he had taken of his kayak and climbing trips. Instead of being a warehouse for the past, Sam had created a highly personal space to which he could retreat.

So it is with most cluttered space. If we move out the stuff that is hogging space we might have room to pause, a place where we can cozy up in a chair to read, or set up a painting easel, or put up a worktable for tying flies.

Purposefully deciding what goes into a space instead of letting it randomly fill up puts us in charge. Lorraine shared these thoughts about her rampage through the bedroom closet when she returned from her Christmas vacation:

"I was having that end-of-the-year crisis when my house and life felt chaotic, so I decided to attack our bedroom. I started with Rick's clothes and pulled everything out. He was a little freaked when he walked into the bedroom and said, 'What the heck are you doing?'

However, once we got it all sorted (he talked me into letting him keep six ugly shirts that he swears he'll only use for camping), we sat back and admired the closet and the fifty or so empty hangers. It looked great, and I felt terrific. Now I knew what was going on in that closet. Then I had a nap and Rick cleaned the rest of the house...now that's a good man!"

A 2000 survey by Ikea showed that 34 percent of us get more satisfaction from cleaning a closet than from sex!

Tanya, Sam, and Lorraine agreed that uncluttered space left more room for them. In such a place they can dream, rest, create, in a word, pause. They also learned this is not about having less, but having more of what resonates with their present life. This means keeping what they actually use: some, but not all, of the mementos of their grandest moments; pictures that catch their breath; books that teach and entertain; vases of lilacs in springtime; and objects they consider beautiful. The liberated space contains comfortable and serviceable furnishings. All the rest is clutter.

Children also need a place to pause, a place that is private and comforting. The ideal child's room should be simply furnished, free from distractions, and clean. An overcrowded, overstimulating environment works against this, as do heaps of toys. Much has been written about the effects of TV on kids, but one thing is clear: television does not belong in a child's bedroom. Choose books instead.

Whether a Queen or a shop clerk, we need somewhere to cast off the stresses of the day—a place that lets us put the worries of the world aside. Coming into a space that is free from brain-bonking distractions and that radiates good feelings from things we love will give us a sense of belonging and harmony. With determination and discipline, we can purge our clutter and begin to transform any environment into one that nurtures our soul, serves our lifestyle, and offers us the perfect place to pause.

Tips to Purge Physical Clutter

- Find a large clutter box for things you don't use
- If you don't wear it, share it. Why clutter your closets (and your life) with clothes you do not use? Let unwanted things go and free up those clogged corners
- If the job is overwhelming, take baby steps. Put aside a few minutes each day and go to it. Be utterly ruthless about bringing anything into your home that does not have a specific purpose. Another word of caution: resist rushing out to purchase organizing bins and storage containers. With less in your home, you will need fewer storage accessories
- Designate a half-day to get started
- Make a quick tour of the house and bag up everything you consider to be garbage
- Start with today's clutter. Deal with current mail. Hang up your clothes. Put in a load of laundry. Clear off the kitchen counters. Recycle newspapers, magazines, flyers, and unnecessary paper immediately. (Give yourself a treat for the great start you have made)
- Select one room, define its purpose, and then remove everything from it that does not support that purpose. This means children's clothes, toys, and school bags go into their rooms; tools go in a toolbox; and coats, hats, mitts, and scarves go into baskets inside the hall closet
- Bag up unused and duplicate items to give to charity
- Get happy. Keep only those things that have a purpose, foster joy, or inspire. Remove anything that stirs negative feelings

- Unclutter surface areas first, and then move into closets and drawers. Take a hint from professional organizers: take everything out and replace only those things you actually use
- If questioning whether to keep an item ask:
    Do I like it?
    Do I really need it? Why?
    Can I replace it if I need to?
    Will I miss it if I let it go?
    Does it belong in this space? If not, put it in a logical place
    When did I last use it? Is it outdated?
    Do I need more than one?
    Does this item trigger negative feelings?
    Does this item bring me joy or inspire me?
- Get tough. Read and recycle newspapers daily. Put outdated magazines in the box for recycling or deliver them to a hospital or another facility. Consider canceling subscriptions in favor of buying issues when you have time to read. If you must retain an article or recipe, clip it out and place it in a file before recycling the publication. If you feel you must keep a book you've read, ask if it will be read again. When?
- Before you bring anything new home, ask yourself if you have a place for it
- Get a clutter-buddy and encourage each other to lighten up!
- Recycle your clutter or put it in the garbage immediately. Unwanted stuff often becomes more storage, or creeps back in the house
- Put on a timer and do a "ten-minute toss" each day. Or find ten clutter culprits to put in the clutter box

- Read *Unclutter Your Life: Transforming Your Physical, Mental,* and *Emotional Space* for solid, practical strategies to create beautiful spaces

Pause to Ponder
- How does your living space make you feel?
- What in it creates these feelings?
- Why are you holding onto things you do not use?
- Are there things in your home you do not like or that create negative feelings?
- If you had more space in your home, how would you use it? As a craft room? A private den?
- How can you allocate the space to make this happen?
- Who would benefit from things you do not use?

Get Organized

*In an orderly environment we can find
what we need in twenty seconds or less.*

"Honey, where did you put my keys?"

*How many times do we hear this plaintive plea (with barely
contained undertones of panic), or ask ourselves such questions
as we whirl through the house, tossing aside sofa cushions,
searching under yesterday's newspapers, and rifling through the
waste bin looking for our keys, wallet, or the kids' summer camp
applications that were due yesterday? Then there is the scramble
as we search for things we are certain we put in a particular spot:
somehow they seem to have grown wings and vanished. The last
time we saw the surface of our desk was when we moved in (and
before we unpacked). And when we reach for the phone, over
tumbles a pile of files. The day has yet to begin!*

A perfect place to pause is clear of clutter, and it is
organized. When we know where things are and can get
them in a jiffy, life flows smoothly instead of in a flurry of
frantic panic attacks. Just as too much stuff generates inner
and outer turmoil so, too, can disorganization turn the most
peaceful human being into a raging tornado. When you are
on a tight schedule, putting things in their place will pay

huge dividends, and perhaps not just the kind you might think. When we have a logical place for our things (and if we discipline ourselves to put things there), we can quickly find what we need.

Searching for misplaced things devours precious weeks of our lives—time we can never retrieve. More than half of us (65 percent in a recent study[27]) say we are extremely busy, yet on average we burn nearly an hour each day looking for things we cannot find. That is almost seven hours a week we could use to practice our golf swing, build sandcastles with the kids, or pause on the patio with tea and a good book.

According to an article in the *Ottawa Citizen*, the average executive wastes 150 hours a year on the job looking for lost or misplaced items. Disorganization costs big-time money. A U.S. knowledge-based company employing 1,000 workers loses on average $48,000 per week ($2.5 million) in time spent locating information.[28]

Creating the perfect place to pause means getting our life's stuff in order, but because are all wonderfully different, our preference for how we organize our environment will vary. Some argue they are the creative types who flourish in a state of "artistic disorder," insisting that in their "system of piles" they know where everything is. I know an event organizer who can juggle a zillion details without a hitch, but stuff is another thing. Her sock drawer harbors pencil sharpeners, and that's where she also tosses dinner invitations and travel brochures. Like many of us, she is highly visual, preferring to see items, rather than to file or store them. Her home is eclectic and filled with mementos of past events, projects on the go, and brochures for upcoming events. Although she might keep a daybook, she is just as likely to jot appointment reminders on scraps of paper. She can function effectively in this environment, but most others would not.

Guy is a talented writer of children's books. His home office doubles as storage space, a workspace, and a catchall for things that do not have a home. It is bursting with his daughter's toys, unfinished projects, and magazines and papers that should be filed or tossed. Somewhere in this mess are writing projects he would like to complete, if he could only find them. For all his good intentions, Guy cannot focus on his work. He admits he resists going into his office, where he is consumed by confusion and feels overwhelmed and defeated. He is sabotaged by his mess, and his office is no place to work, let alone pause.

Getting organized and staying that way frees up significant amounts of time; it also eliminates the frustration and anxiety of feeling out of control. The challenge is to create an environment in which we feel comfortable and can focus energy into productive tasks, as opposed to those laden with anxiety (such as searching for our income tax file or fretting over where we put the first-aid kit). At the end of the day, we can relax with a cappuccino bought with the money saved on late charges we might have paid on bills we could not find. There will be fewer delays and missed appointments. Our relationships will run more smoothly because we show up on time and follow through on commitments. Who knows what opportunities might come our way when others know we are reliable, accountable, and ready to take on new challenges? When our clutter is gone and our things are in order, we are two-thirds of the way towards creating a perfect place to pause.

Tips to Get Organized

If getting organized seems overwhelming, don't despair. Every minute spent organizing reaps dividends in reduced frustration looking for misplaced items, money saved by not purchasing duplicates, and extra time to pause.

Resist the organizing-aid syndrome. Although we might feel a temptation to purchase storage bins, extra shelving, and nifty gadgets, clearing out our clutter will often create extra space. Don't be surprised to find that you need fewer shelves and drawers.

Designate a logical place for everything you own. Searching for misplaced items is a significant time-waster that eats up pause time. Keys, purses, wallets, and eyeglasses are especially prone to "migrating." Put up a key rack near the coat rack and designate a peg for everyone with keys. Keep a mini-toolkit in the laundry room. Encourage everyone to put their belongings in their bedroom or in a logical place. Designate a "business center" for bills, correspondence, and other household papers. Encourage your family to put things back in their place immediately, not "later."

Send the superfluous packing. If something doesn't have a place, ask why. Perhaps it is not something you really need (for example, those cute freebie goodies handed out at trade fairs).

Stop slobbing around. Hang up what you take off. Train yourself and encourage others in your home to put clothes and outerwear in closets.

End the paper chase. Place mail in the "business center" to be opened and dealt with daily. Pay bills immediately or arrange for automatic withdrawal. Establish a file system that is logical to you (color-coded, alphabetical, chronological, by category). Review each file yearly and remove and shred unnecessary documents. Think twice about bringing paper into the house such as concert programs, free pamphlets, brochures, and giveaways.

Don't be a toiletry hoarder. We can reduce time spent in morning grooming by eliminating the clutter-culprits that invade our drawers. Take everything out of the drawers and shelves and eliminate the duplicates and "just-in-case" items. Keep what you actually use. Take special note of expiry dates on medications. Next time you reach for the toothpaste, you will not be grabbing the facial masque you bought when cars still had fins.

If You Need Help

Consider hiring a professional organizer, if only to help you get started. Many are generalists while others specialize in office organization, moving house, paper management, children's rooms, garages, closets, and estates. Engaging a professional offers a practical learning opportunity to stay organized. Professional organizer Linda Chu advises:

"The advantage of engaging the services of a professional organizer is the accountability factor. Like a personal trainer, they keep you focused on your goals and teach you how to get organized to stay that way. Organizing is about identifying the habits that are not working for you and modifying them to create order. Organizing is process-driven, not product-driven. Products only enhance your ability to work and live in a more efficient space. The emphasis still needs to be on how to efficiently go about your day at work and home."

Associations of professional organizers may be found worldwide. In the U.S., look for the National Association of

Professional Organizers (*www.napo.net*); in Canada, the Professional Organizers in Canada may be contacted through the following website: *www.organizersincanada.ca* In Australia, Britain, and other countries, search *www.getorganizednow.com*.

You might also consult the book *Unclutter Your Life: Transforming Your Physical, Mental, and Emotional Space*.

Pause to Ponder
- How do you feel when you can't find what you need?
- What one word describes your organizing ability?
- How much time do you spend searching for misplaced items daily? Weekly? Keeping a log for two weeks will really tell the story.
- What is your greatest barrier to staying organized?
- Which part of your home or workplace is the most disorganized? Why?
- When is the best time to schedule a ten-minute "organizing interval" during the day?

Be a Dusting Diva

When I pause to polish, I dust off my life.

Joseph removes the photographs from the table one at a time. With firm determined strokes he polishes the walnut surface, thinking how fine it looks even with its scars and marks of time. It has been in this room since he and Ellen bought the house more than fifty years ago. She died last spring, but he and the old table are still hanging in — not with the boastful sparkle of youth, but with the mellow sheen of age.

With the polishing done, he examines each photo before setting it in its place. The one in the turquoise frame captures his wife, cheerful and wind-blown on the deck of the boat the couple took to Catalina Island. The photograph with the nick in the corner is a happy reminder of the day his granddaughter, then just a little bit of a thing, reached to touch it and knocked it to the ground. As he replaces each one, his yesterdays live again, and he remembers, and smiles. For him, his weekly routine of cleaning the table and the other things in this room is an act of gratitude, not drudgery at all.

Joseph loves that room even though it would never be featured in *Better Homes and Gardens*. It is filled with the spirit of the people and events that have shaped his life; it is where he comes to rest and be with his thoughts. This is his pause-place. In it he sees the tangible evidence of his life's journey. He tends this room as if it were a shrine, which in many ways, it is.

Such a special room as Joseph's is free from clutter. Everything in it has a reason to be there. It reflects a gentle sense of order. Such a place is tidy, but not painfully perfect; clean, but not sterile. It is a place to be oneself—to pause.

Like Joseph, Maia Gibb considers cleaning precious items a soulful ritual. "Cleaning is a way of appreciating our blessings," says this thirtyish businesswoman who is the inspiration behind The Dusting Divas, a cleaning and de-cluttering service. She believes that hands-on cleaning lets us experience and appreciate our personal space and possessions.

Maia speaks of cleaning as a metaphor for opening space for contentment and new possibilities. "It removes all that is stagnant and negative," she says. Even the ugliest chores take on new meaning under her philosophy. "Stoves and ovens represent abundance. This is where our most nurturing acts take place," she explains. "Keeping them clean and in working order honors their functions. And toilets? When I clean toilets I think of resentments and frustrations and feelings of guilt dissolving and being flushed away. Cleaning a toilet is a great way to purge our problems. Quite therapeutic!" Thinking Maia might be alone in her passion for cleaning toilet bowls, I spoke to another "Dusting Diva," who shared her thoughts.

"I'm having a blast," says Eileen MacNeil, a new Diva who has embraced the clean-with-love ethos. "My work matters." The former sales and marketing expert says her job as a Diva not only gives her great satisfaction, but makes her intensely happy. "I make a difference for my clients by creating joyful, comfortable spaces. And it's great fun. I work with a partner and we sing and joke our way through the day. After one particularly long day when we worked sixteen hours straight, I didn't feel tired. It must have been the aromatherapy in the products we use," she says brightly.

Maia and Eileen are among many who see homes as more than simply places to eat and sleep. They feel we all benefit from having an environment to de-stress, relax, become inspired, and commune with our angels. They emphasize that these spaces deserve the most precious care we can give them. Whether we do the sweeping up or hire someone to help, pausing to lovingly maintain our private spaces not only keeps the dust bunnies at bay, it invites us into a special intimacy with our environment.

Carolyn Bateman, who works from home as a book and magazine editor, shares her thoughts on this: "I think the simple things such as making soup and serving it in a beautiful pottery bowl, waxing a wooden table until it glows, or just sweeping the floor the way the Zen monks do have been overlooked in our high-tech society. That's why I try to practice 'mindfulness'; it helps me experience life, even those parts I might think are mundane." By transforming routine chores into acts of gratitude, she enhances her pleasure in her home and in her special things. It is she who reaps the blessings. What a lovely circle of give and take. And what a lovely way to prepare the perfect place to pause.

Dusting Divas Quickstep
- Put on some great music and get happy
- Open the windows
- Unclutter before you clean
- Toss out grocery bags, dead flowers and plants,

old towels, dated magazines and newspapers
- Do a paper chase. Most of what we keep we do not need
- Start with table and counter surfaces
- Clean top to bottom, left to right
- Clean with care. Your home is your most important environment
- Celebrate with fresh flowers. They bring a room to life.

Green Cleaning Your Perfect Place

Our personal refuges should be free from elements that distract or harm us, mentally or physically. They should be healthful, yet even in the cleanest environments that is not always the case. "The average American household uses forty pounds [of chemical cleaners] each year," says Linda Mason Hunter, author of *Creating a Safe & Healthy Home*.[29] "Cleaning-product manufacturers have turned our near obsession with cleanliness into an $18-million industry that pollutes the environment, harms our bodies, and endangers future generations. Because of the chemicals in many cleaning products, our homes may be more polluted than the outdoors."

This advocate of back-to-the-basics cleaners is shouting out against the toxic products that are poisoning our interior spaces. She cites a 2003 study of chemical residue in household dust that identifies a startling list of dangerous materials. Many commercially produced, all-purpose cleaners may contain toxins such as benzene (a carcinogen) or morpholine, a substance that can harm the liver and kidneys. Certain glass cleaners contain ammonia, a poison that irritates the respiratory system. Fumes from dry cleaning are also environmental culprits that can be absorbed by the body—not exactly what we want in our perfect place to pause.

Did You Know?
- Laundry, dishwashing, and automatic dishwasher soaps that contain phosphates contaminate water systems
- Deodorizers and air fresheners may contain carcinogenic chemicals such as naphthalene and formaldehyde
- Toilet cleaners are the most hazardous products in a home and may contain chlorine and hydrochloric acid
- Traditional dry cleaners use harmful, toxic solvents

Linda's basic cleaning arsenal includes baking soda, vinegar, and soap, her "three graces." She also keeps lemon, washing soda, and castile soap on hand. "Baking soda used with boiling water will keep drains running free," she says. "It's magic for scouring everything from pots to bathtubs, and it costs just pennies. You might need to use a bit more elbow grease than you would with commercial products, but it is worth knowing you're not leaving toxic residues in your home. Regular cleaning with soap and hot water takes care of the germs."

Maia Gibb, who also advocates natural cleaning products, uses essential oils to create healthful environments. She tells us that:

- Lavender is nature's antidepressant. It relaxes us, reduces nervous tension, and works as an antiseptic while cleansing the air. Lavender also repels fleas and mosquitoes.

- Clove oil is excellent for removing molds and is a powerful antiseptic. When inhaled, it relieves exhaustion, and stimulates memory and the respiratory system. Clove oil can also act as a wasp repellent.
- Eucalyptus oil is good for the respiratory system and effective in curbing the effects of asthma. It is also an efficient bug repellent.
- Sweet Orange oil refreshes the air and dissipates bad odors.
- Peppermint oil is an excellent disinfectant. It decongests the sinuses, calms the mind, and soothes headaches.
- Tea Tree oil is a powerful disinfectant, antibacterial, antifungal, and effective treatment for skin problems. It is also non-caustic and non-toxic to the body. It can be used to disinfect any surface, repel odors, and remove molds.

Dry Cleaner Makes a Difference

"Traditional dry cleaners use Perchloroethylene (Perc), a solvent and known human carcinogen that can affect the central nervous system," says Rick Nathorst, owner of Elite Earth-Friendly Cleaners, a company located in Victoria, British Columbia. Solvent-based dry cleaners reuse the same chemicals for multiple loads of clothes because they are expensive. Perc is so toxic that it is considered a hazardous waste. Nathorst's company switched from the traditional system to one that uses water and non-solvent, 100 percent biodegradable additives. Water-based cleaning methods are becoming more common and can now be found in most communities. (Because of the additional expense of installing these systems, the cost to clean an item may be slightly higher.)

The Holland America cruise line is also switching from solvent-based cleaning methods to Elite's process. Within a year of visiting Victoria, Hart Sugarman, who is responsible for the fleet's housekeeping, gave the go-ahead to begin the conversion. Within the first year, four of the cruise line's thirteen ships had been refitted. They plan to refit all new and existing ships. "We'd been searching for a safer method of cleaning. The chemicals we'd been using were highly toxic, deadly, in fact," says Sugarman. "Our new system respects the health of our staff and the environment."

Tips to Clean Green

Below is a list of non-toxic products, common to most households, that make effective cleaners:

- Bicarbonate of soda (baking soda): use for cleaning sinks, toilets, bathtubs, grime, and burnt-on spills. Freshen thermoses with a mixture of one teaspoon of soda and a cup of water.
- White vinegar: mix with water to clean glass, mirrors, ceramic tiles, and floors.
- Lemons: use as a bleach, for odor control, or mix with water to rinse glasses and make them sparkle.
- Biodegradable, non-toxic soap cleans most surfaces.

Recipes for Non-toxic Household Cleaners
Disinfectant Spray
1 tsp borax
2 tbsp vinegar
1/4 tsp dish soap
2 cups very hot water to dissolve ingredients

Dissolve ingredients in the hot water. When the water cools, pour into a spray bottle. Add 1 tsp of grapefruit-seed extract, 30 drops clove, lavender, or Tea Tree oil to make a spray   effective for removing molds.

Air Freshener and Deodorizer
Fill a spray bottle with white vinegar. Add 40-50 drops of your favorite oil. A blend of lavender, mint, and eucalyptus works very well.

Freshen the Fridge
Fill a clean nylon stocking with fresh coffee grounds, or use an opened box of baking soda.

Freshen Carpets
Equal parts baking soda and cornstarch. Add 20 drops of your favorite oil for every cup. Sprinkle on carpet and rub. Let sit for 1 hour or overnight. Vacuum.

Fabric Softener
1/3 cup water, 1/3 cup vinegar and 1/3 cup hair conditioner. Shake, then add to the rinse cycle.[30]

When we adopt an attitude of gratitude for our home base, we will find it easy to give it the care that will create a greater sense of home in us. It will become not just a home, but *our* home—where we find sanctuary from a runaway world, and that vibrates with our own, very special harmony.

Pause to Ponder
- What are your attitudes towards cleaning?
- Contemplate where they originated.
- Do your cleaning products contain toxic ingredients?
- How could you adapt green cleaning strategies for your home, especially your personal retreat space?
- What can you do to make cleaning a positive experience?

Sanctuary Secrets

*An "intentional" environment
harmonizes with our inner journey.*

*Sister Patricia opens the door and greets me with her wide,
lovely smile. While she fetches tea, I wait in the little parlor of her
1920s' Tudor cottage. As I sense the gentle intimacy of the room,
I think, "Ah, this space embraces all who come here." The worn
oak floor and wall paneling glow under soft lamplight. The* Celtic
Benediction, *a book of prayers, and a copy of the* Book of Kells,
*an ancient illuminated manuscript and symbol of Irish
nationalism, rest near the mantle, discreetly disclosing Sister
Patricia's ancestry. A painting of Marie Esther Blondin, the
founder of her order, is also quietly, but prominently displayed,
revealing an anchor in her life.*

*An assortment of comfortable chairs is set about the room.
Two of them are drawn close to a small table, on which I see china
teacups, fresh crusty bread, and strawberry jam. This is a place to
relax and delight in the kindness of a dear friend. When Sister
Patricia arrives with tea, I do just that.*

When we have purged unwanted items, eliminated our
clutter, organized our possessions, and given every corner
a polish and shine, we may be tempted to sit back and

relax. That is fine, but don't get too cozy: creating the perfect place to pause requires a few more steps.

Surroundings That Speak

Our special place could be an entire home or a simple screened-off corner of the living room. Wherever it is, it should offer solitude and comfort and be inspiring. It should exude a welcoming ambience that is uncluttered, organized, and clean. It might be a place we share with others, or that doubles as a guest room or reading room. Whatever area we choose as our domestic pause-place, it should be intensely personal and comforting, and it should reflect who we are.

This ideal environment does not come about by scouring through decorating magazines and then maxing out the credit cards to purchase the latest in home furnishings. It is about digging deep inside to ask how surroundings affect us, how they make us feel, and what we need. We might feel most relaxed in surroundings that harken back to a past era, are filled with cushions and candles, or salute the sleek lines of minimalism. We may want nothing around us at all.

Thoughtfully choosing how we wish to use our space will lead us toward the practical and aesthetic elements required to make it truly ours. Since Sister Patricia's parlor is meant to be a place for intimate conversation and introspection, she desired flexibility and so dismissed the standard two-chairs-and-sofa combination in favor of several comfortable chairs that can either be moved into an intimate setting for two or arranged with others into a larger circle. What furniture will best serve your pause-place?

How Perfect is Your Perfect Place to Pause?

Perhaps you have a place in mind for your
  personal refuge. These questions are offered as
  guides to assess its effectiveness:

- How does this space make you feel? Does it
  invite you in or freeze you out with folded arms
  and a snarl that says "get lost"?
- Is this a private place, a place where other
  people gather, or both? Does your space invite
  you to snooze, read, or think?
- Does it ensure privacy and safety?
- How can you incorporate elements of nature into
  the space?
- Does the space entice you to sit with a friend
  and drink tea with bread and jam?

Elements of a Comforting Environment

Color your world. Much has been written about the psychology of color. Red is said to stimulate appetites and stir feelings of excitement. Green is refreshing. Blues, gentle shades of green, and pinks are soothing, tranquil choices. Choose colors that speak to you, no matter what the current trend might demand.

Lighten up. Creating a cozy environment also requires sunlight. Pull up the blinds and push back the curtains. Mix a solution of water and vinegar to clean the windows and freshen the air. Is there sufficient light for reading? Carefully chosen lamps can double as conversation pieces. Candles are a soothing alternative to traditional lighting.

Go natural. A bouquet of greenery or a bunch of flowers introduces energy and life into a room and reminds us of nature's perpetual beauty. Consider keeping fresh flowers or a plant in your special space. These might range from a container of colorful blooms to a single clipping of holly or spring heather. To my mind, nothing is more wonderful than freesias. I feel certain that these flowers have the scent of heaven.

Put on the ritz. Dismiss the decorators. The perfect place to pause must reflect who *you* are. It should express your sense of aesthetics. Let your life speak in everything you own, from the hanging on the wall to the lamp in the corner.

Create a personal altar. We instinctively create altars in our homes. We might group family photos on a side table or display significant items that center us when we meditate or pray. Stones gathered from places we have been, a piece of art, or a twisted piece of driftwood could form part of an altar. Look about your room. Where is your altar? How can it become a more obvious part of your perfect place to pause?

Pause to Ponder

- What will you be doing in your special place?
- What furnishings do you need to accommodate your needs? Be very specific so as to avoid filling the space with clutter.
- What colors relax you?
- How can you bring the outdoors in?
- What do you need to create a personal altar? Do you already have one?
- How can you harmonize your perfect place to pause with who you are and what you need in your life?

The Perfect Pause

Peace of mind is the ultimate reward of the perfect pause.

Have you ever walked in the gloaming, that mysterious time at dusk when life hovers between day and dark? The light momentarily brightens, hesitates, and then dives into darkness. This brilliant light show is a sign that life really is quite spectacular, if we pause to notice.

Putting the brakes on a runaway life gives us space to immerse our senses in this complex but exquisite planet. It lets us play in an ever-changing wonderland where life's mystery is imbedded in every leaf, rosebud, and wisp of cloud. It lets us experience the gloaming, every day.

Pausing to step outside of our maddening culture allows us to celebrate the immense privilege of simply being alive. For life is a privilege—and it is precious. Let's revel in the delights of life and enjoy our stay!

I have often thought the Garden of Eden refers not to an ancient Biblical paradise, but to the here and now. Eden is ours to enjoy when we stop whirling like windup toys. When we do, we will find it everywhere—in the early-evening sun as it lights the side of a towering building, in the balm of a spring day, the taste of a raindrop, and the sound of children singing. We will be overwhelmed with bliss, for the wonders of Eden surround us constantly.

Pause to play and laugh and marvel, and you will discover that dark clouds can be good and that ant colonies have much to teach you. When we keep life in balance and accept the responsibility that entails, we have time for joy. When we take time to express gratitude for the blessings around us, we connect with our highest self. When we pause to refresh our spirit, we find a place of retreat, whether it is a hut in a mountain hideaway or the corner of a room. We will value our time alone as much as time with those we love. We will recognize the value of silence. We will know that a good sleep and a hearty meal shared with others rejuvenate us better than any double martini.

If we have taken time to pause, then when we come to the end of life we will know we took time to sing and dance to the music in our heart and to love with everything we had. We will have learned that all the money in the world cannot buy peace of mind and that titles and promotions and pats-on-the-back are fun, but a hug from a child is best. We will recall the high points and perhaps shed a tear over the hurtful parts. And if we have kept our body and soul in harmony, and acted with good intentions towards others, we will feel as satisfied as we did after a dinner of roast beef and apple pie.

When we take our final pause, we will know we made time for what mattered most and met our challenges as best we could—that we played our part in this wonderfully complex drama with grace and integrity—that we helped, not impeded, others in their journey. And we will know that Voltaire was right when he said, "Paradise is where I am."

Quick Pauses

1. Take a fifteen-minute walk alone (leave the cellphone behind).
2. Pop into an art gallery at noon.
3. Peruse a magazine before making dinner.
4. Use the good china.
5. Take a lunch break in a park.
6. Goof off.
7. Drop by the library on the way home from work.
8. Turn off the TV and radio and listen to the silence.
9. Abandon the computer for the weekend.
10. Go to bed an hour earlier and read.
11. Sit alone in a garden and examine each petal of a flower.
12. Plant flowers in a pot.
13. Read the Saturday paper from cover to cover.
14. Write in a journal.
15. Pray for fifteen minutes.
16. Take a bus ride and observe the scenery around you.
17. Close your eyes and listen for nature's whispers.
18. Write down the story behind a favorite object you own.
19. Send a note to someone who was kind to you.
20. Smile at a child and hold his gaze.
21. Hold the door for someone.

22. Make a cup of hot chocolate.
23. Eat a prune and buff your brain.
24. Think of five reasons why you are terrific, then write them down.
25. Sing, even if you think you can't.
26. Bake cookies and give them away.
27. Look at a beautiful landscape picture and imagine yourself in it.
28. Put on some music and dance.
29. List five blessings you see around you.
30. Now list five more.
31. And five more.

Keeping in Touch

- Do you have a "pause" story to share?
- Would your organization or company newsletter benefit from an article on pausing?
- Is your association or corporation seeking a motivating and inspirational workshop leader?

Contact Katherine Gibson through
www.katherinegibson.com

Reading List

The following books have guided my thoughts throughout *Pause*. Please enjoy them.

Inner Pauses

Walking for Spirit. Lucinda Vardey. Hidden Springs, 2005.

Living Beauty: Feel Great, Look Fabulous & Live Well. Lisa Petty. Fitzhenry & Whiteside, 2005.

A Pace of Grace. Linda Kavelin Popov. Plume, 2004.

Call To Arms: Embrace a Kindness Revolution. Erik Hansen et al. EWC Press, 2005.

The Power of Appreciation. Noelle C. Nelson and Jeannine Lemare Calaba. Beyond Words Publishing, 2003.

Migration to Solitude. Sue Halpern. Vintage, 1992.

The Delany Sisters Book of Eveyrday Wisdom. Sarah and A. Elizabeth Delany. Kodansha International, 1994.

Forgive for Good. Fred Luskin. Harper SanFrancisco, 2002.

Who Gets Grandma's Yellow Pie Plate: A Guide to Passing on Personal Possessions. University of Minnesota Extension Service, 1999.

Going to Ireland: A Genealogical Researcher's Guide. Sherry Irvine and Nora M. Hickey. Ancestry, 1997.

Your Scottish Ancestry: A Guide for North Americans. Sherry Irvine. Ancestry, 1996.

Your English Ancestry: A Guide for North Americans. Sherry Irvine. Ancestry, 1993.

Scottish Ancestry: Research Methods for Family Historians. Sherry Irvine. Ancestry, 2003.

Finding Your Canadian Ancestors: A Beginner's Guide. Sherry Irvine and Dave Obee. Ancestry, 2007.

Everyday Pauses

The Surprising Power of Family Meals. Miriam Weinstein. Steerforth Press, 2005.

The Mother of All Parenting Books. Ann Douglas. Canadian Edition: Wiley Canada, 2003; U.S. Edition: Wiley, 2004.

Sleep Solutions for Your Baby, Toddler, and Preschooler: The Ultimate No-Worry Approach for Each Age and Stage. Ann Douglas. Wiley, 2006.

Polenta on the Board. Valerie Sovran Mitchell, available at: *www.polenta.ca*

Sleep Thieves. Stanley Coren. Free Press Paperbacks, 1997.

Wanderlust: A History of Walking. Rebecca Solnit. Viking, 2000.

Walking Yoga. Ila Sarley and Garret Sarley. Fireside, 2002.

Walking a Sacred Path: Rediscovering the Labyrinth as a Spiritual Practice. Lauren Artress. Riverhead Trade, 2006

Move Your Body, Tone Your Mood. Kate F. Hays. New Harbinger Publications, 2002.

Healing Family Rifts: Ten Steps to Finding Peace After Being Cut Off from a Family Member. Mark Sichel. McGraw-Hill, 2004.

Playful Pauses

1,000 Places to See Before You Die. Patricia Schultz. Thomas Allen, 2003.

The Therapeutic Garden. Donald Norfolk. Bantam Press, 2000.

Square Foot Gardening. Mel Bartholomew. St. Martins Press, 1981.

Contained Gardens. Susan Berry and Steve Bradley. Ballantine Fawcett, 1995.

Taylor's Guide to Container Gardening. Frances Tenenbaum. Houghton Mifflin, 1995.

Reconnecting with Nature. Michael J. Cohen. Ecopress, 1997.

Voice of the Earth. Theodore Roszak. Simon & Schuster, 1992.

For armchair traveling in Britain, Italy, Spain, and the Holy Lands, look up H.V. Morton. Methuen Publishing, reprints from 2000.

Soulcraft: Crossing into the Mysteries of Nature and Psyche. Bill Plotkin. Thomas Berry New World Library, 2003.

Welcome Home

Unclutter Your Life: Transforming Your Physical, Mental and Emotional Space. Katherine Gibson. Beyond Words Publishing, 2004.

The Emotional House. Kathryn L. Robyn and Dawn Ritchie. New Harbinger Press, 2005.

Spiritual Housecleaning. Kathryn L. Robyn and Dawn Ritchie. New Harbinger Press, 2001.

Creating a Safe & Healthy Home. Linda Mason Hunter. Creative Publishing International, 2005.

Green Clean: The Environmentally Sound Guide to Cleaning Your Home. Linda Mason Hunter and Mikki Halpin. Melcher Media, 2005.

Zen Style: Balance and Simplicity for Your Home. Jane Tidbury. Universe Books, 1999.

The One-Minute Organizer. Donna Smallin. Storey Publishing, 2004.

Your Garagenous Zone: Innovative Ideas for the Garage. Bill West. Paragon Garage Company Ltd. 2004.

Notes

1. "God is Good Medicine," *The Globe and Mail,* 2 April 2002.
2. Veriditas™, 1009 General Kennedy Avenue, 1st Floor, The Presidio, San Francisco, CA 94129-1726 U.S.A.; telephone: (415) 561-2921.
3. For information about *A Pace of Grace* and The Virtues Project go to: *www.paceofgrace.net* and *www.virtues project.com*
4. The home of Centering Prayer, St. Joseph's Abbey in Spencer, Massachusetts, offers retreats for both genders. More at *www.spencerabbey.org* and *www.centeringprayer.com*
5. Statistics Canada General Social Survey, 1998.
6. "It's Official: Statistics Prove We Aren't Getting Enough Sleep," *Victoria Times Colonist,* 9 March 2005.
7. Stefan N. Willich et al., "Noise Burden and the Risk of Myocardial Infarction," *European Heart Journal* 27 (February 2006): beginning 276.
8. *www.quiet.org*
9. For more about quiet gardens, please visit *www.quietgarden.co.uk*
10. Steve MacDowall is the editor of *The Thursday File,* a charming, weekly e-newsletter of inspirational quotations and

newsy information, which I have enjoyed for several years. Its new-subscriber URL is *http://www.thursdayfile. ca/signup.php*

11. U.S. statistics are from the "facts & figures" segment of *www.TVTurnoff.org* an excellent site for learning how to limit television viewing.

12. For more, please refer to *www.puttingfamilyfirst.org*

13. Information from an article by Marion C. Diamond presented to the first joint conference of the Conference of the American Society on Ageing and The National Council on the Ageing, held in New Orleans in March 2001.

14. Robert S. Wilson et al., "Participation in Cognitively Stimulating Activities and Risk of Incident Alzheimer Disease," *JAMA (Journal of the American Medical Association)* 287, no. 6 (13 February 2002): 742-748.

15. "Largest Study of Food Antioxidants Reveals Best Sources," American Chemical Society News Service (6 May 2006).

16. Please see Reading List.

17. Data provided by New York Obesity Research Center of St Luke's-Roosevelt Hospital Center.

18. Based on surveys conducted by the National Sleep Foundation during the years 1999-2004.

19. *www.geocaching.com*

20. J.N. Morris and A.E. Hardman, "Walking to Health," *Sports Medicine* 23, no. 5 (May 1997): 306-332.

21. Health Education Authority (HEA), London. *Health Update 5: Physical Activity*, HEA (1995).

22. Smith A. et al., "The Protective Effects of Physical Exercise on the Development of Alzheimer's Disease." This study released by the American Academy of Neurology at its April 1998 annual meeting in Minneapolis.

23. Michal Artal, with Carl Sherman, "Exercise Against Depression," *The Physician and Sportsmedicine* 26, no. 10

(October 1998): beginning 55.

24. Toronto sports psychologist Kate Hays has written extensively on the psychological benefits of walking. For bibliographical details on her 2002 publication *Move Your Body, Tone Your Mood*, please see Reading List.

25. Research by Rebecca Johnson at the College of Veterinary Medicine's Research Center for Human-Animal Interaction, University of Missouri-Columbia.

26. For more on Henry Vollam Morton's publications, which he began to write in 1925, please see Reading List.

27. Statistic from the National Association of Professional Organizers.

28. *Ottawa Citizen*, 4 January 2003.

29. For bibliographical details, please see Reading List.

30. For more, visit *www.dustingdivas.com*

Index